MW00611823

THE
PRINCESS
BRIDE

THE OFFICIAL COOKBOOK

Jenn Fujikawa

INSIGHT

Smart Pop is an imprint of BenBella Books, Inc.
10440 N. Central Expressway, Suite 800
Dallas, TX 75231
smartpopbooks.com | benbellabooks.com
Send feedback to feedback@benbellabooks.com.

BenBella and *Smart Pop* are federally registered trademarks.

Printed in the United States of America
10 9 8 7 6 5 4 3 2

Library of Congress Control Number: 2022014390
ISBN 9781637741689 (paper-over-board)
ISBN 9781637741696 (electronic)

Editing by Robb Pearlman
Copyediting by Michael Fedison
Proofreading by Karen Wise and Brock Foreman
Indexing by Amy Murphy Indexing Services, Inc.
Text design and composition by Kit Sweeney
Cover design by Brigid Pearson
Printed by Versa Press

**Special discounts for bulk sales are available.
Please contact bulkorders@benbellabooks.com.**

Contents

GF = Gluten-Free · V = Vegetarian · V+ = Vegan

THE GRANDFATHER: I brought you a special present.

THE GRANDSON: What is it?

THE GRANDFATHER: Open it up.

THE GRANDSON: A book?

THE GRANDFATHER: That's right. When I was your age, television was called books. And this is a special book. It was the book my father used to read to me when I was sick, and I used to read it to your father. And today, I'm gonna read it to you.

Introduction

Storytelling is how we pass down information. It's communication at its finest, allowing the listener to use their own imagination and the storyteller to put forth their best efforts to paint an audible picture. There's nothing more comforting than a good old-fashioned fairy tale. These fanciful stories fill our minds with the wonder and intrigue of dashing heroes, dastardly villains, thrilling adventures, and yes, even some romance.

Storytelling creates a special bond, the shared details that can only be experienced between the storyteller and the listener. It's why everyone has their own versions of the same tale; the nuance of the narrator, and their relationship with the listener, makes all the difference.

Cooking for your family is much like storytelling. You pass down information, adding your own special flair to each recipe, knowing that, in the end, the special ingredient is always love. It's the same closeness that makes traditional family recipes so special.

The Princess Bride is that perfect recipe of humor, drama, adventure, and romance, which is why it lends itself so well to themed food recipes. Cooking along while reciting your favorite quotes or reenacting memorable scenes is what makes the experience of creating film-related dishes so enjoyable.

The Princess Bride debuted in movie theaters in 1987, introducing now iconic lines like "As you wish" and "Inconceivable!" Viewers laughed at the comedy of errors that befell our heroes, were awed by a frightening world that gave us R.O.U.S.es (rodents of unusual size), and were charmed by the love story of Westley and Buttercup.

Based on William Goldman's 1973 novel, *The Princess Bride*, the film has captivated fans of all ages throughout the years with its witty storytelling and adventurous action. The film's impact was recognized when the movie was inducted into the National Film Registry in 2016.

Director Rob Reiner and his crew made Florin a reality, while the perfectly cast performances brought the characters to life. Peter Falk as the caring Grandfather anchors the story as he reads a classic tale to his sick grandson, played by a young Fred Savage. Like most children, the Grandson is irritated at first by his grandfather's doting, but he is soon won over by the engrossing narrative of Westley and Buttercup's adventures.

Intertwining with the world of the Grandfather and the Grandson is a remarkable cast whose legacy will forever be tied to the fabulous fairy tale. Robin Wright's Buttercup was steadfast in her belief in true love, while the dashing heroics of Cary Elwes's Westley made audiences rally behind his cause. Andre the Giant played the literal giant Fezzik, who was expertly paired with his revenge-seeking counterpart, Inigo Montoya, played by Mandy Patinkin. Chris Sarandon's Prince Humperdinck and Christoper Guest's Count Rugen were villains you'd want to root against, while Wallace Shawn's memorable Vizzini and magic-makers Billy Crystal and Carol Kane brought lighthearted fun at just the right moments.

This cast enchanted audiences who watched this fantasy world come to life through a grandfather's narration to his grandchild. The dynamic of Falk's grandpa telling the story in detail to his stay-at-home sick grandson played by Savage made the story leap off the page, as if we the audience were the ones at home, cuddled in our bed eating soup and waiting to hear what happens next. Watching the film, we all became the grandson, willing to tolerate a cheek-pinching grandpa's affections to hear a tale of heroics, danger, and love.

This cookbook captures the film's universality, and its feeling of comfort through storytelling. The recipes reflect the best-loved qualities of our beloved characters. Fezzik's strength, Inigo's courage, Westley's wits, and Buttercup's stoicism provide the foundation for meals that will bring the audience into the world of *The Princess Bride* through food.

The recipes are edibly immersive, allowing you to feel as if you were living in the story yourself. The worlds of Florin and Guilder become tangible through these flavors, and let you set the stage for a themed party or picnic, all through fanciful dishes.

In the end it's wove, twoo wove, that will have you wanting to make these recipes for your own family and friends.

THE GRANDSON: Has it got sports in it?

THE GRANDFATHER: Are you kidding? Fencing. Fighting. Torture. Revenge. Giants. Monsters. Chases. Escapes. True love. Miracles.

THE GRANDSON: It doesn't sound too bad. I'll try and stay awake.

Chapter One

Enchanting Breakfasts

ew children who love video games and sports want to spend the day stuck in bed. And fewer still would want to spend their time listening to their grandfather read them a book. So it's understandable that the Grandson is less than thrilled when his grandfather cracks open a copy of *The Princess Bride*, by S. Morgenstern. But the magic of storytelling will soon change the Grandson's mind.

As the Grandfather's descriptions morph into the on-screen striking landscape of Florin, moviegoers cannot help but also be swept away by the beauty of seeing his words coming to life. You can almost smell breakfast cooking on Buttercup's farm. And as the fresh dairy, recently harvested eggs, and sizzling meats are prepared, we imagine Westley working to finish the chores Buttercup has assigned him.

The old saying is true—breakfast really is the most important meal of the day. It sets you up for how you're going to tackle the world. And whether you're on a farm, in a city, or on the high seas, morning meals should be easy, as carefree as possible after a long night's sleep.

These enticing breakfast recipes will start off your day of adventure.

THE GRANDFATHER: Buttercup was raised on a small farm in the country of Florin . . . Her favorite pastimes were riding her horse and tormenting the farm boy that worked there. His name was Westley, but she never called him that . . . Nothing gave Buttercup as much pleasure as ordering Westley around.

BUTTERCUP: Farm boy. Polish my horse's saddle. I want to see my face shining in it by morning.

WESTLEY: As you wish.

BUTTERCUP: Farm boy. Fill these with water—please.

WESTLEY: As you wish.

THE GRANDFATHER: That day, she was amazed to discover that when he was saying "As you wish," what he meant was "I love you." And even more amazing was the day she realized she truly loved him back.

BUTTERCUP BUTTERMILK SCONES

Growing up on her family's farm, Buttercup was no stranger to hard work. There were horses to be groomed, cows to be milked, and daily chores that were all made much easier with the help of the "farm boy." Bossing him around was a job in itself, but all necessary to get the newly harvested farm ingredients. Fresh buttermilk, cream, and butter are the key to making these fluffy, light scones. The ideal early morning meal to start off a day of farm work, they're best served with a bit of fresh jam and homemade clotted cream, but you can serve them "as you wish."

MAKES 12 SERVINGS (V)

- 2 cups all-purpose flour
- ¼ cup granulated sugar
- 2 teaspoons baking powder
- ¼ teaspoon kosher salt
- ½ cup (1 stick) cold unsalted butter, cubed
- 1 large egg, lightly beaten
- ½ cup buttermilk
- 2 teaspoons vanilla extract
- ¼ cup heavy cream
- 1 tablespoon sanding sugar
- Jam, for serving
- Clotted cream, for serving

1. Preheat the oven to 400°F. Prep a baking sheet with parchment greased with nonstick spray.
2. In a large bowl, whisk together the flour, granulated sugar, baking powder, and salt.
3. Work the butter into the flour mixture, until crumbly.
4. Stir in the egg, buttermilk, and vanilla, until just combined.
5. Scoop ¼-cup portions of dough 2 inches apart onto the prepped baking sheet.
6. Brush the scones with the heavy cream. Sprinkle with the sanding sugar.
7. Bake for 18 minutes, until lightly browned. Transfer to a wire rack and let cool slightly.
8. Serve with jam and clotted cream.

Hash You Wish

"As you wish." No words have ever carried more weight than those three declared by Westley to the love of his life, Buttercup. Whatever her command, he dutifully obeys. Taking care of one's every wish is quite an undertaking and requires sustenance to get through a day of chores. This morning medley of hearty potatoes, meaty bacon, and succulent beef is fried up and topped with beautifully runny eggs, giving you the nourishment you need to tackle any obstacles that might come your way and endanger your beloved.

MAKES 4 SERVINGS (GF)

HASH

2 medium russet potatoes, peeled and diced
5 strips of bacon, diced
1 small onion, diced
1 garlic clove, minced
2 cups diced Fire Swamp Boiled Beef (page 81)

2 cups fresh spinach leaves
1 teaspoon kosher salt
½ teaspoon dried basil
½ teaspoon paprika
¼ teaspoon black pepper
1 tablespoon minced fresh parsley

EGGS

1 tablespoon unsalted butter
4 large eggs
½ teaspoon kosher salt
¼ teaspoon black pepper

1. *To make the hash:* Place the potatoes in a large pot and cover with 1 inch of water. Bring to a boil over medium-high heat. Reduce the heat and simmer for 4 to 5 minutes, until tender.

2. In a large skillet over medium-high heat, add the bacon and cook for 8 to 10 minutes, until crispy. Remove and drain.

3. Add the onion and garlic to the bacon grease in the skillet and cook for 3 to 4 minutes, until softened.

4. Add the beef, potatoes, and spinach. Stir in the salt, basil, paprika, and pepper. Cook for 10 minutes, until the potatoes are crispy and the spinach has wilted. Fold the bacon back in and cook for another 5 minutes.

5. Sprinkle with the parsley, and set aside.

6. *To make the eggs:* In a separate skillet over medium heat, melt the butter, then crack the eggs into the pan.

7. When the edges of the eggs start to turn white, cover the pan and lower the heat. Cook for 4 minutes, until the whites firm up. Season with the salt and pepper.

8. Serve the eggs with the hash.

Farm Boy Breakfast

Who would have thought working on a modest farm in Florin would lead to pirating the seas as the Dread Pirate Roberts? It's those humble beginnings that prepared Westley for a life of buccaneering. Westley's love for Buttercup kept him going, just like when he tackled his never-ending farm tasks. But he never would have been able to do anything had he not started his day with an ample breakfast of homemade fluffy biscuits topped with a mouthwatering sausage gravy. This robust meal is the ideal start to any day, whether you're working on the farm or sailing out into the open sea.

— MAKES 6 SERVINGS —

BISCUITS
2 cups all-purpose flour, plus more for dusting
1 tablespoon baking powder
2 teaspoons granulated sugar
½ teaspoon kosher salt

6 tablespoons cold unsalted butter, cut into cubes
¾ cup buttermilk
1 tablespoon melted unsalted butter

GRAVY
8 ounces ground breakfast sausage

1 teaspoon rubbed sage
1 teaspoon dried thyme
2 tablespoons unsalted butter
3 tablespoons all-purpose flour
1½ cups whole milk
½ teaspoon kosher salt
½ teaspoon black pepper

1. *To make the biscuits:* Preheat the oven to 425°F. Prep a baking sheet with parchment.
2. In a large bowl, whisk together the flour, baking powder, sugar, and salt.
3. Work the cold butter into the flour mixture and rub together until it resembles a coarse meal.
4. Mix in the buttermilk until just combined.
5. Turn the dough out onto a lightly floured surface and pat out to 1 inch thick.
6. Fold the dough in half, turn it, and pat it out again. Do this for a total of 5 times to create layers.
7. Use a 3-inch round cutter to cut out circles.
8. Place onto the prepped baking sheet and brush with the melted butter.
9. Bake for 14 to 15 minutes, until golden brown. Let cool on a wire rack.
10. *To make the gravy:* In a medium skillet over medium heat, cook the sausage, sage, and thyme, until the sausage has browned.
11. Stir in the butter, until melted.
12. Sprinkle in the flour and cook for 2 to 3 minutes, until combined.
13. Whisk in the milk, and bring to a simmer. Whisk constantly for 1 to 2 minutes, until thickened.
14. Season with the salt and pepper, and serve over the biscuits.

Prince Humperdinck's Eggs and Soldiers

Prince Humperdinck, a man of incredible power and bearing, is so tyrannical, so vile, there's no rival when it comes to his nefarious treachery. As skilled as he is in villainy, he's equally masterful in war. What morning repast would be suitable for a man of such ruthlessness? Why, soft-boiled eggs, of course. These breakfast staples served with toast are reminiscent of soldiers on parade and thusly named, making them the quintessential meal for a man with impeccable tracking abilities and a death wish for his bride-to-be.

— Makes 1 serving (V) —

2 large eggs
¼ teaspoon kosher salt

⅛ teaspoon black pepper
2 slices multigrain bread

1 tablespoon unsalted butter

1. Place the eggs in a saucepan and cover with 1 to 2 inches of water. Turn on the heat to medium-high and bring to a boil.
2. Turn off the heat, cover with a lid, and let sit for 4 to 5 minutes.
3. Use a slotted spoon to transfer the eggs to egg cups. Tap the top of the eggs with a spoon to crack, then remove the shell. Slice off the tops, then season with the salt and pepper.
4. Toast the bread and spread with butter. Cut into strips.
5. Dip the toast strips into the egg to serve.

COUNT RUGEN: Your Princess is really a winning creature. A trifle simple, perhaps, but her appeal is undeniable.

PRINCE HUMPERDINCK: Oh, I know. The people are quite taken with her. It's odd, but when I hired Vizzini to have her murdered on our engagement day, I thought that was clever. But it's going to be so much more moving when I strangle her on our wedding night. Once Guilder is blamed, the nation will be truly outraged. They'll demand we go to war.

BRUTE SQUAD BAKE

Having to clear out Thieves' Forest of its unsavory inhabitants is no easy feat; it's a Herculean task that requires only the strongest and bravest of men. That's where the Brute Squad comes in. There is no dangerous situation they can't handle. Their intimidation tactics are always on point. Rallying for such an undertaking requires the squad to be at their peak, and this savory bake is made with one dozen eggs—no more, no less—and will give them just the strength they need to enforce the will of Prince Humperdinck.

— MAKES 8 SERVINGS (GF) —

12 large eggs
¼ cup whole milk
1 teaspoon dried basil
1 teaspoon dried parsley
½ teaspoon onion powder

4 strips of bacon, diced
1 shallot, minced
1 cup cherry tomatoes, halved
1 cup fresh spinach leaves

¼ teaspoon kosher salt
¼ teaspoon black pepper
½ cup shredded cheddar cheese

1. Preheat the oven to broil.
2. In a large bowl, whisk together the eggs, milk, basil, parsley, and onion powder. Set aside.
3. In a large ovenproof skillet over medium-high heat, add the bacon and cook for 6 to 7 minutes, until crispy. Remove and set aside to drain.
4. Add the shallot to the bacon grease in the skillet and cook for 2 minutes, until softened.
5. Stir in the tomatoes and spinach and cook for 1 to 2 minutes, until the spinach has wilted.
6. Pour over the egg mixture, then add the bacon. Season with the salt and pepper.
7. Sprinkle the cheese on top and cook for 2 to 3 minutes, until the edges are just set.
8. Transfer the skillet to the oven and broil for 2 to 3 minutes, just until the eggs are set in the middle, then serve.

> MIRACLE MAX: Beat it or I'll call the Brute Squad.
>
> FEZZIK: I'm on the Brute Squad.
>
> MIRACLE MAX: You are the Brute Squad.

Kissing Book Brioche

Brioche is a traditional bread made with love, often made from family recipes handed down and enjoyed through the generations, much like the Grandfather handing down the story of The Princess Bride *to his grandson. Like the fable being told, the bread is only a piece of a larger story. Add a little milk, some sugar, and spice, and everything starts to come together.*

While this breakfast dish and the story seem simple at first glance, they're both actually multilayered, delightfully sweet, and enchanting enough in their complexity to keep you coming back for more.

— MAKES 4 SERVINGS (V) —

2 large eggs
¾ cup whole milk
1 tablespoon packed
  light brown sugar
1 teaspoon vanilla extract
1 teaspoon ground

cinnamon
¼ teaspoon ground nutmeg
¼ teaspoon kosher salt

2 tablespoons unsalted
  butter
8 slices brioche bread
1 tablespoon
  confectioners' sugar
Maple syrup, for serving

1. In a shallow dish, whisk the eggs, milk, brown sugar, vanilla, cinnamon, nutmeg, and salt. Set aside.
2. In a skillet over medium heat, melt the butter.
3. Dip a slice of bread quickly into the egg mixture, coating both sides.
4. Place the bread in the skillet and cook for 3 to 4 minutes on each side, until golden brown. Repeat with the rest of the bread.
5. Sift over the confectioners' sugar.
6. Serve with syrup.

THE GRANDSON: Is this a kissing book?

THE GRANDFATHER: Wait, just wait.

THE GRANDSON: Well, when does it get good?

THE GRANDFATHER: Keep your shirt on, and let me read.

Silver Dollar Fortune Seeking Pancakes

Westley loved Buttercup but had no money for marriage. What's a poor farm boy to do but leave to find his fortune across the sea? If only Westley had known what was ahead of him on that journey. Before leaving the love of his life and departing on such an uncertain quest, this meal of mini mouthwatering flapjacks shaped like an abundance of wealth would surely bring him the luck he'd need to find prosperity, so that he could come back and reunite with his true love, riches in hand.

MAKES 8 SERVINGS (V)

2 cups all-purpose flour
3 tablespoons granulated sugar
2 teaspoons baking powder

½ teaspoon ground cinnamon
¼ teaspoon ground nutmeg
¼ teaspoon kosher salt
1½ cups whole milk

½ cup sour cream
1 large egg
1 teaspoon grated lemon zest

1. In a large bowl, whisk together the flour, sugar, baking powder, cinnamon, nutmeg, and salt.

2. Make a well in the center of the dry ingredients and stir in the milk, sour cream, egg, and lemon zest, until just combined.

3. Heat a nonstick skillet over medium-low heat. Ladle ¼-cup circles of batter into the pan. Cook for 3 to 4 minutes. When small bubbles appear and begin to pop, flip the pancakes over and cook for another 2 minutes, until cooked through and golden brown. Repeat to make the remaining pancakes, and serve.

GUILDER'S PEACEFUL PORRIDGE

Guilder, the sworn enemy of Florin, was just minding their own business when they almost got roped into the scheme Humperdinck masterminded to wage war between the two nations. Vizzini undertook this task—after all, starting a war is a prestigious line of work with a long and glorious tradition. The rival country was such an unknowing pawn in the whole ploy, one can imagine they'd just be peacefully enjoying a morning bowl of warm porridge with not a care in the world, only to be caught up in dreadful subterfuge, all before lunch. Poor, unsuspecting Guilder.

MAKES 4 SERVINGS (GF, V+)

1 cup steel-cut oats
2½ cups almond milk
2 tablespoons packed light brown sugar
½ teaspoon vanilla extract

½ teaspoon ground cinnamon
¼ teaspoon ground nutmeg
¼ teaspoon kosher salt
½ cup fresh blackberries

¼ cup chopped pecans
2 tablespoons edible flowers

1. In a large saucepan, stir together the oats, almond milk, brown sugar, vanilla, cinnamon, nutmeg, and salt. Bring to a boil, then reduce the heat to a simmer. Cook for 5 to 7 minutes, until thickened.

2. Spoon into serving bowls. Top with the blackberries, pecans, and edible flowers and serve.

PRINCESS CROWN BREAKFAST TART

Florin law gave Prince Humperdinck the right to choose his bride, and because tales of her beauty were known far and wide, he chose a commoner, Buttercup. From the outside, she looked the part—regal, beautiful—but alas, she did not love him. Anything can be dressed up to be worthy of royalty, even this morning tart. Crowned with heavenly mascarpone cream and fresh vibrant fruit, it's a meal truly fit for a princess. Even a heartbroken princess waiting for her true love to return can't resist such royal fare.

— MAKES 8 SERVINGS (V) —

CRUST
½ cup (1 stick) unsalted butter
½ cup packed light brown sugar
1 large egg
1 tablespoon maple syrup
½ teaspoon vanilla extract
1 cup granola

¾ cup all-purpose flour
½ teaspoon ground cinnamon
¼ teaspoon kosher salt

FILLING
8 ounces cream cheese, softened
1 cup confectioners' sugar
2 tablespoons lemon juice

1 tablespoon grated lemon zest
1 cup heavy cream

TOPPING
1 cup blueberries
1 cup sliced mango
1 cup raspberries
1 kiwi, peeled and sliced
¼ cup apricot preserves

1. *To make the crust:* Preheat the oven to 350°F. Prep a 9-inch tart pan with nonstick spray.
2. In the bowl of an electric mixer, cream the butter and brown sugar, until fluffy.
3. Stir in the egg, until just combined.
4. Stir in the maple syrup and vanilla, until combined.
5. Stir in the granola, flour, cinnamon, and salt.
6. Press the mixture into the prepped tart pan. Cover with parchment and weigh down with pie weights. Bake for 15 minutes, until golden brown. Let cool.
7. *To make the filling:* In a medium bowl, stir together the cream cheese, confectioners' sugar, lemon juice, and lemon zest. Set aside.
8. In a large bowl with a hand mixer, whip the heavy cream, until stiff peaks form.
9. Fold the cream cheese mixture into the whipped cream. Pour into the cooled crust, spreading evenly.

continued on next page

continued from previous page

10. *To prepare the topping:* Arrange the blueberries, mango, raspberries, and kiwi in concentric circles on top of the tart.
11. In a small bowl, microwave the apricot preserves for 15 to 30 seconds, until slightly warmed. Brush the preserves as a glaze over the fruit.
12. Refrigerate the tart until ready to serve.

BUTTERCUP: Oh, Westley, will you ever forgive me?

WESTLEY: What hideous sin have you committed lately?

BUTTERCUP: I got married. I didn't want to. It all happened so fast.

WESTLEY: Never happened.

BUTTERCUP: What?

WESTLEY: Never happened.

BUTTERCUP: But it did! I was there. This old man said "man and wife."

WESTLEY: But did you say "I do"?

BUTTERCUP: Um, no. We sort of skipped that part.

WESTLEY: Then you're not married. You didn't say it. You didn't do it.

MOST LIKELY KILL YOU IN THE MORNING

When you're acting as the valet for the Dread Pirate Roberts, every day on the high seas might be your last. Therefore, it's best to welcome each morning thankful that you made it through the night. This morning-time meal has an equally ominous name and is full of flavor with just the right kick. Known as eggs in purgatory, this skillet of fresh eggs is nestled into a bed of spicy goodness made of tomatoes, peppers, and paprika, which gives it its devilishly delicious appearance. This mouthwatering meal is a great way to wake up to the relief that you're still alive.

MAKES 6 SERVINGS (GF, V)

2 tablespoons olive oil
1 medium onion, diced
2 garlic cloves, minced
2 tablespoons tomato paste
1 can (28 ounces) crushed tomatoes

1 red bell pepper, diced
1 teaspoon paprika
1 teaspoon ground cumin
½ teaspoon red pepper flakes
½ teaspoon kosher salt

¼ teaspoon black pepper
6 large eggs
4 ounces feta cheese, crumbled
1 teaspoon chopped fresh parsley

1. In a large skillet over medium-high heat, add the olive oil, onion, and garlic. Cook for 4 to 5 minutes, until softened.

2. Stir in the tomato paste, crushed tomatoes, and red bell pepper. Season with the paprika, cumin, red pepper flakes, salt, and black pepper. Lower the heat to low and simmer for 10 minutes.

3. Use the back of a spoon to create 6 wells in the sauce, then crack an egg into each well. Cover with a lid and cook for 5 minutes, until the whites are set.

4. Remove from the heat, sprinkle with the feta and parsley, and serve.

Chapter Two

Gallant Lunches

good meal can do wonders for relationships. Over an engaging lunch, alliances can form, misunderstandings can be reconciled; there's nothing that can't be resolved over a bountiful midday meal. Eating with friends opens up conversations, creating a catalyst for open discussions and jovial tales that only true comrades can share. Perhaps you'll find out that your friend has a lifelong revenge plan and he's been honing his skills for years, or that another pal has a particular gift for rhyming.

INIGO: That Vizzini, he can . . . fuss.

FEZZIK: . . . fuss . . . fuss . . . I think he likes to scream at us.

INIGO: Probably he means no harm.

FEZZIK: He's really very short on charm.

INIGO: Oh, you've a great gift for rhyme.

FEZZIK: Yes, some of the time.

Journeying out on the water for years at a time can be quite the bonding experience. Fezzik and Inigo formed an unbreakable bond; they shared hopes and dreams, looked out for one another, and shared many meals while floating amongst the waves. Even Prince Humperdinck and Rugen have an evil brotherhood bond that few can understand. When your right-hand man quite literally has six fingers on his right hand, there's an unspeakable intimacy that will make you follow through with villainous plans without question.

As in life, just like friends, the lunch you choose says a lot about you. Hearty and loyal or light and laughable, lunching with friends is the ultimate in camaraderie. Eating. Fencing. Fighting. Torture. Revenge. Giants. Monsters. Chases. Escapes. True love. Miracles. What more could a group of good pals ask for?

Six-Fingered Sandwiches

At just eleven years old, Inigo decided to dedicate his life to fencing, to avenge his father's death and find the six-fingered man who killed him. After twenty years, asking every swordsman you encounter how many fingers they have on their right hand can be a little repetitive, to say the least. While the search continues, you can always count on a good finger sandwich. Creamy herbed butter combined with fresh crunchy cucumbers on soft-as-silk bread is just what you need to continue on the road to vengeance. At least you know these finger sandwiches definitely won't betray you.

Makes 4 servings (V)

HERBED BUTTER
½ cup (1 stick) salted butter, softened
1 tablespoon chopped fresh dill
1 teaspoon chopped fresh thyme
1 teaspoon grated lemon zest

SANDWICHES
8 slices soft white bread, crusts trimmed
1 cup sliced English cucumber
4 sprigs fresh dill

1. *To make the herbed butter:* In a small bowl, stir together the butter, dill, thyme, and lemon zest.
2. *To prepare the sandwiches:* Spread the herbed butter onto 4 of the bread slices.
3. On the other 4 bread slices, lay the cucumber on top, then the dill. Place the remaining bread slices on top, buttered-side down.
4. Cut each sandwich into three rectangles and serve.

INIGO: My father was slaughtered by a six-fingered man. He was a great sword maker, my father. And when the six-fingered man appeared and requested a special sword, my father took the job. He slaved a year before he was done.

MAN IN BLACK: I have never seen its equal.

INIGO: The six-fingered man returned and demanded it, but at one-tenth his promised price. My father refused. Without a word, the six-fingered man slashed him through the heart. I loved my father, so, naturally, challenged his murderer to a duel. I failed . . .

MAN IN BLACK: How old were you?

INIGO: I was eleven years old. When I was strong enough, I dedicated my life to the study of fencing. So the next time we meet, I will not fail. I will go up to the six-fingered man and say, "Hello, my name is Inigo Montoya. You killed my father. Prepare to die."

CHIPS OF INSANITY

The sheer rock face of the Cliffs of Insanity is an incomparable challenge, but Fezzik attempts it with the Man in Black not far behind. To be fair, Fezzik is doing it while carrying three people. Nonetheless, the precipice is a mighty beast, similar to this towering serving of teetering chips. Much like Fezzik attempting the climb, these are loaded up with extra accoutrements. Melted cheese, fresh tomato and avocado, tangy sour cream, and just enough jalapeños to heighten the experience makes these just as precarious as the Cliffs themselves.

MAKES 6 SERVINGS (GF)

4 strips of bacon
8 ounces potato chips
2 cups shredded cheddar
  cheese

1 medium tomato, diced
1 avocado, peeled, pitted,
  and sliced
¼ cup sour cream

¼ cup sliced jalapeños

1. Preheat the oven to 400°F.
2. In a skillet over medium-high heat, cook the bacon for 8 to 10 minutes, until crispy. Crumble and set aside.
3. Line a baking sheet with parchment. Repeatedly layer the potato chips and cheddar cheese on the prepped baking sheet. Bake for 10 minutes, until the cheese has melted.
4. Top with the crumbled bacon, tomato, avocado, sour cream, and jalapeños and serve.

MLT—"Mutton," Lettuce, and Tomato Sandwich

> **MIRACLE MAX:** Sonny, true love is the greatest thing in the world. Except for a nice MLT, a mutton, lettuce, and tomato sandwich, where the mutton is nice and lean and the tomato is ripe. They're so perky. I love that.

Miracle Max's confidence may be taking a dive thanks to Prince Humperdinck, but there's one thing he confidently knows and it's that true love is the greatest thing in the world. He also knows sandwiches. A nice MLT—a mutton, lettuce, and tomato sandwich—is pretty hard to beat, too. A three-ingredient combination that is a trio of triumph. While fresh mutton may not be readily available near your hovel, substitute a few slices of succulent roast beef. When the beef is nice and lean and the tomato is ripe? Now that's true love.

Try a vegetarian version where mushrooms make for a tasty stand-in!

—————— MAKES 4 SERVINGS ——————

SAUCE
- ½ cup Greek yogurt
- 1 garlic clove, minced
- 1 tablespoon chopped fresh parsley
- 1 tablespoon lemon juice
- ¼ teaspoon ground cumin
- ¼ teaspoon kosher salt
- ¼ teaspoon black pepper

FILLING
- 1 tablespoon olive oil
- 1 small shallot, sliced
- 1 garlic clove, minced
- 1 pound thinly sliced roast beef (or 1 pound sliced white mushrooms)
- ½ teaspoon onion powder
- ¼ teaspoon black pepper

SANDWICHES
- 4 slices provolone cheese
- 4 split buns
- 4 to 6 iceberg lettuce leaves
- 1 medium tomato, sliced
- 1 small red onion, sliced

1. *To make the sauce:* In a small bowl, stir together the Greek yogurt, garlic, parsley, lemon juice, cumin, salt, and pepper. Refrigerate until ready to use.
2. *To make the filling:* In a skillet over medium heat, add the olive oil and cook the shallot and garlic for 2 minutes, until softened.
3. Add the roast beef (or mushrooms, if using). Season with the onion powder and pepper. Cook for 3 to 4 minutes, until warmed through.
4. *To prepare the sandwiches:* Place the provolone on the buns and top with the warm roast beef. Add the lettuce, tomato, and red onion. Drizzle with the sauce and serve.

MOSTLY DEAD

According to Miracle Max, there's a big difference between mostly dead and all dead. Mostly dead is still slightly alive; therefore, you still have something worth fighting for. Now, a dish that is mostly dead, well, it's not like you want to battle with it on the plate—but a little sear never hurt anyone. This seared ahi packs a flavorful punch with the addition of tangy soy sauce and a combination of black and white sesame seeds, giving it the perfect crunch in opposition to its fresh interior. This dish won't fight back, but it will give your taste buds a run for their money.

MAKES 4 SERVINGS

2 tablespoons soy sauce
1 teaspoon packed light
  brown sugar

1 teaspoon sesame oil
4 (6-ounce) tuna steaks
¼ cup black sesame seeds

¼ cup white sesame seeds
2 tablespoons olive oil

1. In a small bowl, whisk the soy sauce, brown sugar, and sesame oil. Pour over the tuna.
2. Mix the sesame seeds in another shallow dish, then press the tuna into them to coat.
3. Heat the olive oil in a large skillet over high heat. Place the tuna in the skillet and sear for 45 seconds on each side.
4. Slice and serve.

INIGO: He's dead. He can't talk.

MIRACLE MAX: Look who knows so much. Well, it just so happens that your friend here is only mostly dead. There's a big difference between mostly dead and all dead. Please open his mouth . . . Now, mostly dead is slightly alive. Now, all dead . . . well, with all dead, there's usually only one thing that you can do.

INIGO: What's that?

MIRACLE MAX: Go through his clothes and look for loose change.

THE GIANT'S BOULDERS

Fezzik is quite good at throwing boulders with deadly precision. When faced with an adversary like the Man in Black, he knows he can take him out quickly, but where's the fun in that? These fabulously weighty rounds are similar in heft to the boulders the giant lifts with ease, but instead these are filled with gooey and delicious mac and cheese. Fried to perfection, these edible boulders have a flavor that is sure to knock you off your feet.

———— MAKES 8 SERVINGS (V) ————

MAC AND CHEESE
1 pound elbow macaroni
2 tablespoons unsalted butter
2 tablespoons all-purpose flour
1 can (12 ounces) evaporated milk

3 cups grated cheddar cheese
½ teaspoon seasoned salt
¼ teaspoon black pepper

FRYING
3 cups bread crumbs
1 tablespoon dried oregano

2 teaspoons dried basil
2 teaspoons onion powder
1 teaspoon garlic salt
½ teaspoon black pepper
1 quart vegetable oil
2 large eggs, beaten
2 cups marinara sauce

1. *To make the mac and cheese:* Cook the macaroni according to the package instructions. Drain and set aside.
2. In a large pot over medium-high heat, add the butter and flour and whisk for 2 minutes, until thickened. Stir in the milk and cheese, until melted.
3. Fold in the cooked macaroni, salt, and pepper.
4. Pour into a 13 x 9-inch pan and let cool slightly, then refrigerate for 2 hours.
5. Use a large scoop to shape the mac and cheese into balls and place on a baking sheet. Freeze for 6 to 8 hours.
6. *To prepare the fried ingredients:* In a shallow dish, mix the bread crumbs, oregano, basil, onion powder, garlic salt, and pepper.
7. In a large, deep skillet, heat the oil to 350°F.
8. Dip the mac and cheese balls into the beaten eggs, then roll in the bread crumb mixture, until covered.
9. Fry for 4 to 5 minutes, until golden brown. Let drain on a wire rack.
10. Serve with the marinara sauce.

FEZZIK: What do I do?

VIZZINI: Finish him, finish him. Your way.

FEZZIK: Oh, good, my way. Thank you, Vizzini . . . Which way is my way?

VIZZINI: Pick up one of those rocks, get behind the boulder, and in a few minutes, the Man in Black will come running around the bend. The minute his head is in view, hit it with the rock!

FEZZIK: My way's not very sportsmanlike.

Unemployed in Greenland

To hear Vizzini tell it, when he found Fezzik, he was friendless, brainless, helpless, hopeless, and unemployed in Greenland. To be fair, the brawny, lovable giant would've been just fine, as he always seems to be able to get himself out of a bad situation. But when one's without gainful employment, food options can be slim. This tangy tuna salad is light yet robust and served on delicate lettuce leaves, but still packs enough of a protein punch for even the biggest brawler in all the land.

MAKES 4 SERVINGS (GF)

- 2 cans (6 ounces) tuna packed in water, drained
- 1 celery rib, minced
- 1 tablespoon minced shallot
- ¼ cup mayonnaise
- 1 tablespoon pickle relish
- 1 teaspoon Dijon mustard
- ¼ teaspoon onion powder
- ¼ teaspoon kosher salt
- ¼ teaspoon black pepper
- 4 large butter lettuce leaves

1. In a large bowl, mix together the tuna, celery, shallot, mayonnaise, relish, Dijon mustard, onion powder, salt, and black pepper.
2. Spoon into lettuce cups and serve.

FEZZIK: I just don't think it's right, killing an innocent girl.

VIZZINI: Am I going mad or did the word "think" escape your lips? You were not hired for your brains, you hippopotamic landmass.

INIGO: I agree with Fezzik.

VIZZINI: Oh. The sot has spoken. What happens to her is not truly your concern—I will kill her. And remember this, never forget this—when I found you, you were so slobbering drunk you couldn't buy brandy. And you—friendless, brainless, helpless, hopeless. Do you want me to send you back to where you were, unemployed in Greenland?

THE GRANDSON'S SOUP AND SANDWICH

When you're not feeling well, there's nothing quite like curling up in bed with a good book and lunch. And there's no better cure-all than a soup and sandwich. This good old-fashioned bowl of piping-hot chicken noodle soup is accompanied by a grilled cheese sandwich, but like the tale being told by the Grandfather to the Grandson, there's more to this sandwich than meets the eye. The secret weapon in this side dish, aside from true love, is a thin layer of pastrami, which adds just enough flavorful zest to nurse you back to health.

— MAKES 4 SERVINGS —

SOUP
1 tablespoon olive oil
1 pound boneless, skinless chicken thighs, diced
½ teaspoon kosher salt
½ teaspoon black pepper
1 tablespoon unsalted butter
1 large onion, diced
2 garlic cloves, minced
3 celery ribs, chopped

3 medium carrots, chopped
1 tablespoon dried oregano
1 tablespoon dried thyme
1 teaspoon onion powder
1 bay leaf
10 cups chicken broth
2 teaspoons lemon juice
8 ounces dried wide egg noodles

2 tablespoons chopped fresh parsley

SANDWICHES
8 thin slices pastrami
½ cup (1 stick) unsalted butter, softened
8 slices sourdough bread
½ teaspoon garlic powder
1 cup shredded Gruyère cheese
1 cup shredded Swiss cheese

1. *To make the soup:* Place a large pot over medium heat. Add the olive oil and chicken, seasoning with salt and pepper. Cook for 2 to 3 minutes, until browned. Remove and set aside.

2. Into the same pot, add the butter and cook the onion, garlic, celery, carrots, oregano, thyme, onion powder, and bay leaf for 5 minutes, until soft.

3. Pour in the chicken broth and lemon juice, and bring to a boil. Lower the heat and return the chicken to the pot. Cover and simmer on low for 20 minutes, until the chicken is cooked through. Scoop off and discard the foam.

4. Add the noodles and cook for 8 minutes, until tender. Sprinkle with the parsley.

5. *To prepare the sandwiches:* In a large skillet over medium heat, warm the pastrami until crispy. Transfer to a plate and set aside.

continued on next page

continued from previous page

6. Spread the butter onto one side of each slice of bread. Sprinkle with the garlic powder and place 4 of the slices, buttered-side down, in the same skillet over medium-low heat. Top with half the cheese, the pastrami, then the rest of the cheese. Place the remaining bread on top, buttered-side up. Cook for 3 to 4 minutes, until the cheese starts to melt. Flip over and cook for another 3 to 4 minutes, until browned and the cheese has melted.

7. Slice the sandwiches in half and serve with the soup.

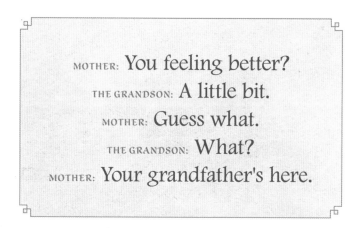

MOTHER: You feeling better?

THE GRANDSON: A little bit.

MOTHER: Guess what.

THE GRANDSON: What?

MOTHER: Your grandfather's here.

R.O.U.S.es

If you think R.O.U.S.es don't exist, this recipe is going to come as quite a surprise. These Rolls of Unusual Size are savory pastries and are much more endearing than their unpleasant counterparts—the Rodents of Unusual Size—that hang around the Fire Swamp. While they can still be classified as unusually sized, these are filled with an addicting ham and cheese combo, conveniently travel well, and are easy to take on a long journey. Don't worry, they still have quite a bite!

— MAKES 8 SERVINGS —

1 cup warm milk (110°F)
1 package (.25 ounce) active dry yeast
4 tablespoons (½ stick) unsalted butter, melted
1 tablespoon honey

3 cups all-purpose flour, plus more for dusting
½ teaspoon kosher salt
1 tablespoon olive oil
¾ cup diced smoked ham
1 cup shredded Gruyère cheese

16 sliced almonds
16 small raisins
1 egg plus 1 tablespoon water, for egg wash
¼ cup grated Parmesan cheese

1. In the bowl of an electric mixer fitted with the dough hook, stir together the milk, yeast, butter, and honey. Let sit for 10 minutes, until the yeast starts to bubble.
2. With the mixer on low, gradually add the flour and salt, until just combined. With the speed on medium, knead the dough for 5 minutes, until smooth and elastic.
3. Place the dough in a large bowl greased with olive oil. Cover with plastic wrap. Let rise for 1½ hours, until the dough has doubled in size.
4. Punch down the dough. Divide the dough into 8 balls. Place on a parchment-lined baking sheet and cover with a tea towel. Let rest for 20 minutes.
5. Flatten out a ball of dough and place some ham and cheese in the center. Pull up the edges to seal. Form into a teardrop shape, pulling the excess dough on one end and rolling out into a long tail, then pressing the end back into the body of the roll. Repeat with the remaining dough balls, ham, and cheese.
6. Add 2 sliced almonds, pointed side down, to create the ears, and add 2 raisins for the eyes. Place 2 inches apart back on the parchment-lined baking sheet. Cover with a tea towel, and let rise for another 30 minutes.
7. Preheat the oven to 350°F.
8. Brush the dough balls with the egg wash and sprinkle with the Parmesan. Bake for 20 minutes, until lightly browned. Serve.

WESTLEY: I mean, what are the three terrors of the Fire Swamp? One, the flame spurts. No problem. There's a popping sound preceding each—we can avoid that. Two, the Lightning Sand. But you were clever enough to discover what that looks like, so in the future we can avoid that, too.

BUTTERCUP: Westley, what about the R.O.U.S.es?

WESTLEY: Rodents of Unusual Size? I don't think they exist.

WESTLEY: I told you I would always come for you. Why didn't you wait for me?

BUTTERCUP: Well . . . you were dead.

WESTLEY: Death cannot stop true love. All it can do is delay it for a while.

⚜ Chapter Three ⚜
Adventurous
Dinners

Dinner is a time to wind down at the end of the day with friends and family. It's a moment to catch up and get updates on everyone's lives, and take the time to listen and have meaningful conversations. Food is the bond that brings people together, and there's nothing better than good food shared with good friends. It's also the perfect time to regale one another with well-told stories, whether they be historic in nature or maybe a few tall tales just for show.

THE GRANDSON: Who kills Prince Humperdinck? At the end, somebody's got to do it. Is it Inigo? Who?

THE GRANDFATHER: Nobody. Nobody kills him. He lives.

THE GRANDSON: You mean he wins? Jesus, Grandpa! What did you read me this thing for?

THE GRANDFATHER: You know, you've been very sick and you're taking this story very seriously. I think we better stop now.

THE GRANDSON: No! I'm okay. I'm okay. Sit down. All right?

THE GRANDFATHER: Okay. All right, now, let's see. Where were we? Oh yes. In the Pit of Despair.

Dinner is when a normal recounting of the day has the opportunity to turn into a wild revelation from a mundane recount and trigger an outrageous scenario. A well-prepared meal can help embellish narratives simply through smell and taste.

And if you're having dinner solo, there's no better dinner companion than a good book or a captivating movie. Stories and food go hand in hand, and themed meals can pull you into the world of gallant heroes, dazzling daredevils, and wistful romance, and make you feel like you're part of the action. Maybe just skip the iocane-laced beverages, to be safe.

Whether it's a candlelight dinner for two or a large family-size potluck, a hearty repast coupled with an enchanting story can turn an evening meal into a memorable affair.

BONETTI'S DEFENSE

As Inigo duels with the Man in Black, he quickly recognizes he's met an equal match. Battling with a fellow skilled swordsman, Inigo realizes he's being outmatched by the fencing move known as Bonetti's defense, named after fencing master Rocco Bonetti. When it comes to swordsmanship, there's nothing quite like a mouthwatering meaty skewer; wielded with precision and grilled over a hot flame, they're poised and ready for action. These succulent kebabs are all that you need to prepare you for the fight of your life.

MAKES 4 SERVINGS

1 pound beef sirloin, cut into 1-inch cubes
¼ cup olive oil, plus more for oiling the grill
2 garlic cloves, minced
2 tablespoons soy sauce

2 tablespoons Worcestershire sauce
1 teaspoon dried basil
1 teaspoon paprika
¼ teaspoon kosher salt
¼ teaspoon black pepper

1 green bell pepper, cut into thick chunks
1 sweet onion, cut into thick chunks
Additional supplies: 4 to 6 metal or wooden skewers

1. In a sealable bag, add the beef, olive oil, garlic, soy sauce, Worcestershire sauce, basil, paprika, salt, and pepper. Marinate for 6 hours in the refrigerator.
2. If using wooden skewers, soak in water for 20 minutes before grilling.
3. Preheat the grill to 375°F. Lightly grease with oil.
4. Skewer the beef, bell pepper, and onion onto the skewers. Grill for 12 to 15 minutes, turning in between.

INIGO: You're using Bonetti's defense against me, ah?

MAN IN BLACK: I thought it fitting, considering the rocky terrain . . .

INIGO: Naturally, you must expect me to attack with Capo Ferro.

MAN IN BLACK: Naturally—but I find Thibault cancels out Capo Ferro, don't you?

INIGO: Unless the enemy has studied his Agrippa . . . which I have.

SHRIEKING EELS

That high-pitched shrieking sound you hear? Those are the Shrieking Eels. Native to the waters between Florin and Guilder, you won't want to find yourself alone at sea with those monsters of the deep. Luckily, the only screams you'll hear with this bowl of brackish broth are screams of joy with each warm spoonful. Here, there are no watery creatures to fear—the elongated forms are simply thick udon noodles, waiting to be scooped up and eaten in the warm miso broth. Perfect for days at sea when you're trying to avoid the murky waters below.

VIZZINI: Do you know what that sound is, Highness? Those are the Shrieking Eels—if you doubt me, just wait. They always grow louder when they're about to feed on human flesh.

You can find udon noodles, dashi granules, miso paste, kamaboko, and nori in the Asian aisle of the grocery store.

— MAKES 2 SERVINGS —

NOODLES

2 packages (7 ounces) udon noodles

SOUP

4 cups chicken broth

2 teaspoons dashi granules
¼ cup white miso paste
1 tablespoon soy sauce
1 tablespoon sugar
1 teaspoon sesame oil

TOPPINGS

2 green onions, diced
6 slices kamaboko (fish cake)
¼ cup shredded nori (dried seaweed)

1. *To make the noodles:* Bring a medium pot of water to a boil. Add the udon noodles and cook for 2 to 3 minutes. When the noodles loosen, drain the noodles but do not rinse. Set aside.

2. *To make the soup:* In a medium saucepan over medium-high heat, bring the chicken broth and dashi granules to a boil.

3. In a small bowl, stir together the miso paste and ½ cup of the boiling dashi water, stirring until the miso has dissolved. Pour the mixture back into the pot. Reduce the heat to medium, and stir in the soy sauce, sugar, and sesame oil; simmer for 2 to 3 minutes.

4. *To finish with the toppings:* Divide the noodles between two bowls, then ladle over the soup. Garnish with the green onions, kamaboko, and shredded nori and serve.

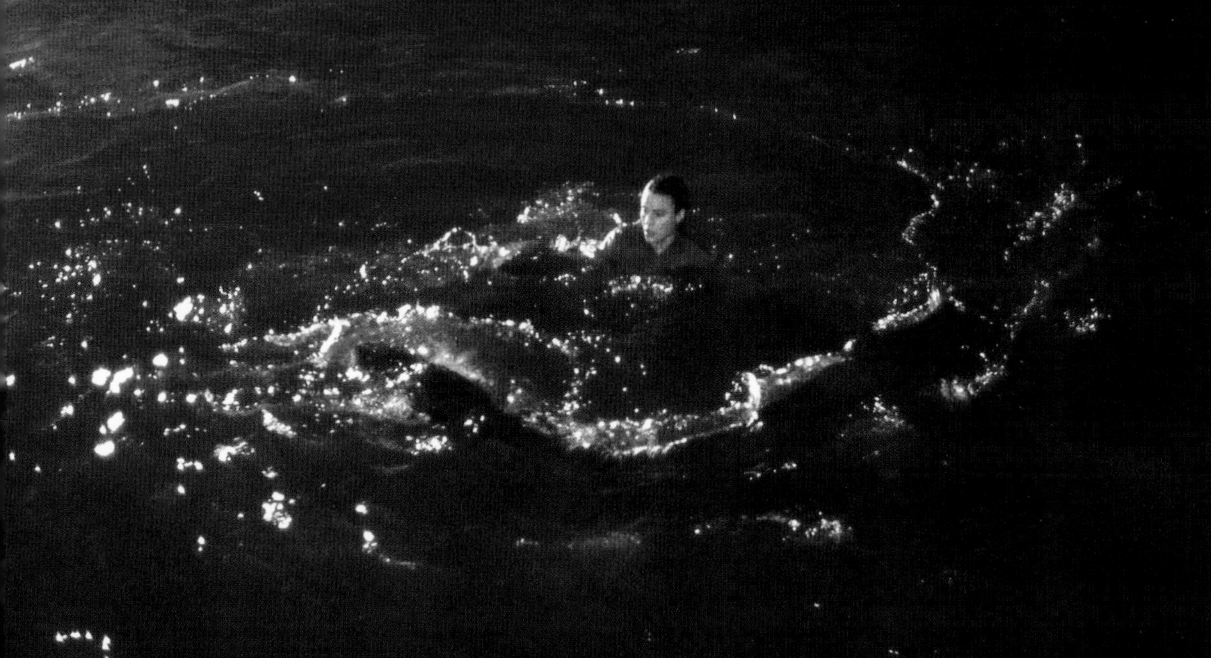

SPANIARD'S PAELLA

A Spaniard traveling the precarious seas must get a little melancholy, longing for home. This flavorful paella is reminiscent of Inigo's homeland. It's a visually enticing dish and a seafood lover's dream. Made in a special pan, it's piled high with fragrant saffron rice and plenty of glorious ocean catches, like succulent shrimp, tender clams, and briny mussels, that all come together in a beautiful seafaring party. Not to worry, you'll find no Shrieking Eels here. This abundant plato del día will quell homesick thoughts and fuel you for a long journey ahead.

MAKES 8 SERVINGS (GF)

3 tablespoons olive oil
1 medium onion, diced
1 small green bell
   pepper, diced
2 garlic cloves, minced
¼ cup dry white wine
1 can (14 ounces) diced
   tomatoes
1 pound boneless, skinless
   chicken thighs, cubed

6 ounces chorizo, sliced
   into rounds
1 cup short-grain paella
   rice
1 pinch saffron threads
2 teaspoons sweet
   paprika
½ teaspoon kosher salt
¼ teaspoon black pepper
4 cups chicken broth

8 ounces large shrimp,
   shelled (tails left on)
   and deveined
8 ounces clams, scrubbed
   and rinsed
8 ounces mussels,
   scrubbed and debearded
½ cup peas
1 lemon, cut into wedges
2 tablespoons chopped
   fresh parsley

1. In a 15-inch paella pan over medium heat, add the olive oil and cook the onion, bell pepper, and garlic for 5 minutes, until softened and translucent.

2. Pour in the wine and cook for 1 to 2 minutes. Stir in the tomatoes with their juices.

3. Add the chicken and chorizo and cook for 3 to 4 minutes, until the chicken is browned.

4. Stir in the rice, saffron, paprika, salt, and pepper. Gently stir in the chicken broth, and bring to a boil. Lower the heat and simmer for 20 minutes.

5. Nestle the shrimp, clams, and mussels into the rice. Cook for 10 minutes more, until the shrimp is cooked through and the clams and mussels have opened (discard any that do not open).

6. Stir in the peas and add the lemon wedges to the pan. Sprinkle with the parsley and serve.

VIZZINI: You fell victim to one of the classic blunders. The most famous is "Never get involved in a land war in Asia." But only slightly less well-known is this: "Never go in against a Sicilian when death is on the line."

Vizzini's Sicilian Meatballs

Have you ever heard of Plato? Aristotle? Socrates? Morons. Only a fool would want to match wits with Vizzini. The Sicilian has a short temper, but he knows what's what when it comes to conniving and manipulation. A battle of wits is bad enough, but in the battle of traditional meals, being outmatched by tantalizing Italian flavors is hardly a fair fight. Studded with currants and pine nuts, these distinctive meatballs honor the Sicilian tradition of blending and highlighting the unique, classic flavors of southern Italy. Too good to pass up—I'd say this round goes to Vizzini.

MAKES 6 SERVINGS

2 slices white bread
⅓ cup whole milk
1½ pounds ground beef
1 large egg, beaten
2 garlic cloves, minced
2 teaspoons chopped fresh parsley, plus more for serving

1 teaspoon dried marjoram
1 teaspoon dried oregano
½ teaspoon kosher salt
½ teaspoon black pepper
⅓ cup currants
¼ cup pine nuts

¼ cup grated Parmesan cheese, plus more for serving
3 tablespoons vegetable oil
1 jar (28 ounces) marinara sauce

1. Tear the bread into pieces and place in a small bowl with the milk. Set aside to soften.

2. In a large bowl, add the ground beef, beaten egg, garlic, parsley, marjoram, oregano, salt, pepper, currants, pine nuts, Parmesan cheese, and softened bread. Mix together until just combined. Form into 18 equally sized meatballs.

3. In a skillet, heat the oil and cook the meatballs until browned on all sides, about 5 minutes.

4. Add the marinara sauce to the skillet and simmer for 30 minutes, until cooked through.

5. Garnish with parsley and Parmesan and serve.

FEZZIK'S STEW

When Inigo heads back to Thieves' Forest to wait for Vizzini, he's in bad shape. Fezzik, ever loyal, nurses his inebriated friend back to health, telling him of Vizzini's death and, more important, the existence of Inigo's longtime nemesis Count Rugen, the six-fingered man. To get Inigo ready for the fight of his life, Fezzik feeds him a hearty bowl of stew. Cooked for hours to get the full flavor of the herbs and a little bit of wine for good measure, this stew will get you back into fighting shape. There's nothing quite like slow-cooked meat and veg to get you back into the business of revenge.

MAKES 6 SERVINGS (GF)

1½ pounds cubed stew meat
1 teaspoon kosher salt
½ teaspoon black pepper
2 tablespoons olive oil
1 can (28 ounces) diced tomatoes
4 cups beef broth
1 cup dry red wine

1 tablespoon Worcestershire sauce
8 ounces pearl onions, peeled
1 tablespoon dried oregano
1 tablespoon dried rosemary
1 tablespoon dried thyme
1½ teaspoons dried mustard

1 bay leaf
3 large carrots, cut into chunks
4 large celery ribs, cut into chunks
1 pound red potatoes
2 tablespoons cornstarch
2 tablespoons minced fresh parsley

1. Season the meat with the salt and pepper.
2. In a Dutch oven, heat the olive oil over medium-high heat.
3. Brown the beef on all sides. Remove from the pot and set aside.
4. Add the tomatoes with their juices, beef broth, red wine, and Worcestershire sauce. Bring to a boil.
5. Lower the heat to low. Return the meat to the pot, along with the pearl onions, oregano, rosemary, thyme, mustard, and bay leaf. Simmer for 1 hour.
6. Add the carrots, celery, and potatoes. Simmer for 45 minutes.
7. In a small bowl, make a slurry by whisking together the cornstarch and a few tablespoons of the stewing liquid. Stir the slurry into the stew and simmer for 10 minutes, until the stew has thickened.
8. Discard the bay leaf. Garnish with the parsley and serve.

Thieves' Forest Flatbread

Thieves' Forest is not the most picturesque of places, what with its nefarious inhabitants, danger around every corner, and whatnot. Only the Brute Squad has the tenacity to go in and lay down Humperdinck's law. The forest is filled with pockets of interesting, unique characters at every turn, much like this tasty flatbread. Salty prosciutto and plump tomatoes are encased in gooey mozzarella and protected by a forest of arugula. With ambrosial flavors in every bite, it's much like Thieves' Forest—you never know what you'll happen upon next.

— MAKES 6 SERVINGS —

16 ounces refrigerated or thawed frozen pre-made pizza dough
1 tablespoon extra-virgin olive oil
1 tablespoon grated Parmesan cheese

1 garlic clove, minced
1 cup shredded mozzarella cheese
½ cup thinly sliced red onion
½ cup cherry tomatoes, halved

4 ounces prosciutto, torn
1 cup arugula
¼ cup feta cheese, crumbled
1 tablespoon balsamic vinegar

1. Preheat the oven to 425°F. Prep a baking sheet with parchment paper.
2. Roll the dough out into a 12 x 15-inch rectangle. Place on the prepped baking sheet. Brush the dough with the olive oil and sprinkle with the Parmesan and garlic.
3. Sprinkle on the mozzarella cheese. Top with the red onion, cherry tomatoes, and torn prosciutto. Bake for 15 minutes, until the crust is browned and the prosciutto is crispy.
4. Top with the arugula and feta cheese. Drizzle over the balsamic vinegar and serve.

WESTLEY: Ha. Your pig fiancé is too late. A few
more steps and we'll be safe in the Fire Swamp.
BUTTERCUP: We'll never survive.
WESTLEY: Nonsense—you're only saying that
because no one ever has.

FIRE SWAMP BOILED BEEF

The Fire Swamp is a dark and treacherous place. Nobody who has entered has ever survived. Full of unexpected and sometimes exploding dangers, the Fire Swamp certainly keeps you on your toes—especially if the hem of your gown catches fire. This boiled beef has just as much heat and layers of intrigue. And though there are no Rodents of Unusual Size in this cauldron of brisket, you can certainly add your own R.O.U.S.es (page 56) as a side dish.

MAKES 6 SERVINGS (GF)

3 pounds beef brisket
1 tablespoon packed
   light brown sugar
1 tablespoon ground
   cloves
1 tablespoon mustard
   seed
1 tablespoon peppercorns

1 tablespoon kosher salt
1 bay leaf
2 garlic cloves, minced
8 cups water
1 tablespoon apple cider
   vinegar
2 pounds small red
   potatoes

2 large carrots, peeled and
   cut into 2-inch chunks
3 celery ribs, cut into
   2-inch chunks
1 large onion, cut into
   quarters
1 medium head cabbage,
   cut into wedges

1. In a large pot, add the brisket, brown sugar, cloves, mustard seed, peppercorns, salt, bay leaf, and garlic. Pour in the water and apple cider vinegar and bring to a boil. Cover and turn the heat down to low; simmer for 2½ hours.

2. Add the potatoes, carrots, celery, and onion. Cover and simmer for another 45 minutes.

3. Add the cabbage and cook for another 15 minutes, until softened.

4. Discard the bay leaf. Slice the beef and serve.

THE IMPRESSIVE CLERGYMAN: Mawidge . . .
mawidge is what bwings us togewer
today . . . Mawidge, the bwessed
awwangement, that dweam
wiffim a dweam.

MAWIDGE MEATWOAF

"Mawidge . . . mawidge is what bwings us togewer today." The Impressive Clergyman performing the ceremony to marry Buttercup and Humperdinck certainly has a way with words, words that are a little hard to understand. But this meatwoaf is crystal clear as far as creating a delicious meal for your bwessed awwangement. Made with a mawidge of beef and pork, flavored with herbs, and topped with a sweet and tangy spread, it's a solid foundation for a new beginning. A twoo union of holy matwimony of fwavors.

MAKES 6 SERVINGS

1 tablespoon olive oil
1 pound ground beef
1 pound ground pork
1 cup diced onion
1 garlic clove, minced
½ cup panko bread crumbs
1 large egg, beaten

1 tablespoon
  Worcestershire sauce
1 teaspoon dried basil
½ teaspoon dried oregano
½ teaspoon paprika
½ teaspoon kosher salt
¼ teaspoon black pepper

½ cup ketchup
1 tablespoon yellow
  mustard
1 tablespoon packed light
  brown sugar

1. Preheat the oven to 375°F. Lightly grease a loaf pan with the olive oil.

2. In a large bowl, combine the ground beef, ground pork, onion, garlic, panko, egg, Worcestershire sauce, basil, oregano, paprika, salt, and pepper.

3. Press the mixture into the loaf pan. Bake for 1 hour.

4. In a small bowl, stir the ketchup, mustard, and brown sugar together. Spread on top of the meatloaf.

5. Bake for another 10 minutes, until the ketchup mixture is bubbly and the internal temperature reaches 160°F.

6. Let rest for 5 minutes. Slice and serve.

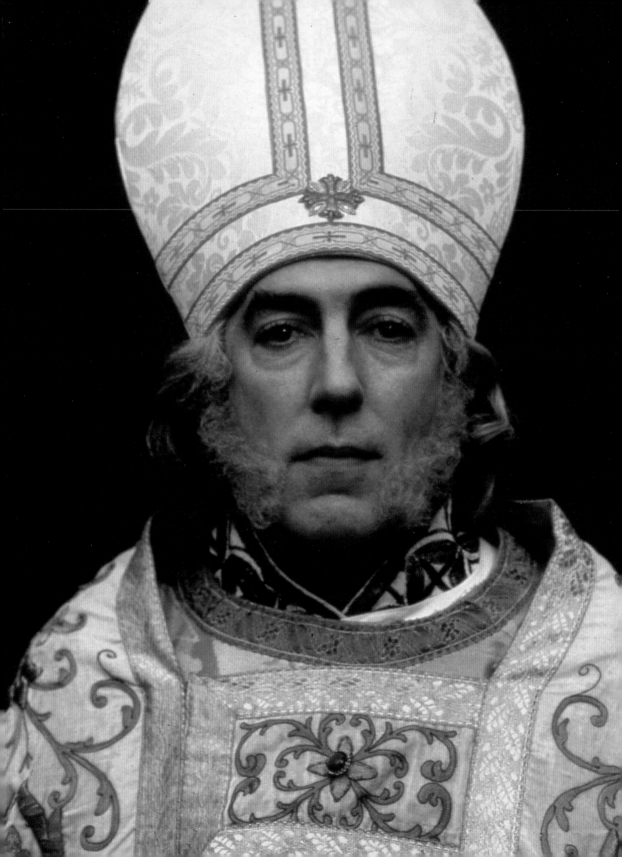

HAVE YOU THE WING

It takes a truly gifted orator to perform a sacred wedding ceremony for the soon-to-be king of Florin. And despite Humperdinck's insistence to hurry the service along, the Impressive Clergyman won't be swayed from taking his sweet time. When he asks, "Have you the wing?" it's easy to misunderstand that he may be asking for a succulent piece of poultry rather than the band that signifies a holy bond. These aromatic wings will make you forget the murderous intent of your betrothed and are best when eaten with your true soul mate by your side.

MAKES 4 SERVINGS (GF)

2 pounds chicken wings
1 tablespoon olive oil
2 tablespoons cornstarch
2 tablespoons confectioners' sugar

1 tablespoon chili powder
1 tablespoon sweet smoked paprika
1 teaspoon garlic powder

1 teaspoon onion powder
1 teaspoon kosher salt
1 teaspoon black pepper

1. Preheat the oven to 400°F. Place a wire rack on a baking sheet, and grease with nonstick spray. Set aside.
2. In a large bowl, toss the chicken wings with the olive oil.
3. In a sealable plastic bag, add the cornstarch, confectioners' sugar, chili powder, paprika, garlic powder, onion powder, salt, and pepper.
4. Add the chicken wings and shake to coat. Place on the prepped rack on the baking sheet. Bake for 45 minutes, until cooked through. Serve.

VALERIE'S PORTABLE POCKET PIES

When it's a miracle you need, Miracle Max and his wife, Valerie, are your go-to problem solvers. Valerie's indomitable spirit and love of love makes her the perfect complement to Max's crankiness. Once the two fix you up and set you on your path, you might be sent off with these magical portable pocket pies. Here's where the magic happens—use leftover Fezzik's Stew (page 75) as filling and you'll be done in no time. Full of meaty goodness and substantial enough for a long journey, these pastries will keep you steady so you can have fun storming the castle.

MAKES 8 SERVINGS

1 package (2-count) refrigerated or thawed frozen pie dough

3 to 4 cups chopped leftover Fezzik's Stew (page 75)

1 large egg plus 1 tablespoon water, for egg wash

½ teaspoon kosher salt

1. Preheat the oven to 400°F. Prep two baking sheets with parchment.

2. Divide the dough into 8 equal pieces, then roll out into circles. Add 2 to 3 tablespoons of filling in the center of each round. Brush the edges with the egg wash. Fold the crust over the filling, pressing the edges to close. Use the tines of a fork to seal the edges. Place on the prepped baking sheets. Cut two small slits into the top of the dough to vent.

3. Brush the tops with more egg wash. Sprinkle with the salt. Bake for 15 minutes, until golden brown. Serve.

WESTLEY: What are our liabilities?

INIGO: There is but one working castle gate . . .
and it is guarded by sixty men.

WESTLEY: And our assets?

INIGO: Your brains, Fezzik's strength, my steel.

Chapter Four

Swashbuckling Snacks

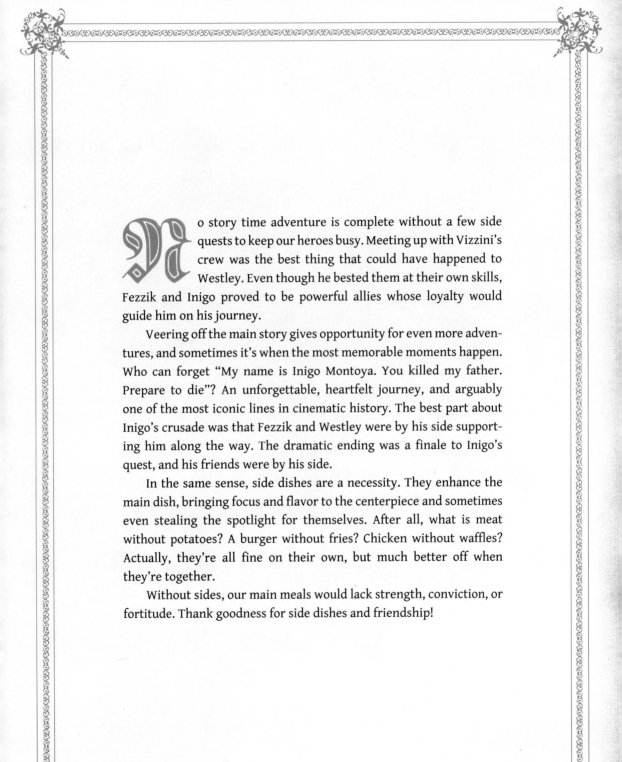

No story time adventure is complete without a few side quests to keep our heroes busy. Meeting up with Vizzini's crew was the best thing that could have happened to Westley. Even though he bested them at their own skills, Fezzik and Inigo proved to be powerful allies whose loyalty would guide him on his journey.

Veering off the main story gives opportunity for even more adventures, and sometimes it's when the most memorable moments happen. Who can forget "My name is Inigo Montoya. You killed my father. Prepare to die"? An unforgettable, heartfelt journey, and arguably one of the most iconic lines in cinematic history. The best part about Inigo's crusade was that Fezzik and Westley were by his side supporting him along the way. The dramatic ending was a finale to Inigo's quest, and his friends were by his side.

In the same sense, side dishes are a necessity. They enhance the main dish, bringing focus and flavor to the centerpiece and sometimes even stealing the spotlight for themselves. After all, what is meat without potatoes? A burger without fries? Chicken without waffles? Actually, they're all fine on their own, but much better off when they're together.

Without sides, our main meals would lack strength, conviction, or fortitude. Thank goodness for side dishes and friendship!

WESTLEY'S WITS

In a battle of wits, Westley is unrivaled. His cleverness has saved his life many times, and it's all thanks to his quick thinking. Add Fezzik and Inigo, and you have quite the triple threat. Every squad can use a little help when it comes to shrewd intellect, and consuming certain ingredients can actually stimulate your brain. This crunchy, healthy salad is filled with foods like kale and walnuts, which are key components for developing the intellectual capacity perfect for focusing on your team's strengths.

MAKES 6 SERVINGS (GF)

DRESSING
- ¼ cup white wine vinegar
- 2 tablespoons lemon juice
- 1 tablespoon Dijon mustard
- 1 tablespoon honey
- 1 garlic clove, peeled

- 1 tablespoon dried oregano
- 1 teaspoon kosher salt
- ¼ teaspoon black pepper
- ½ cup extra-virgin olive oil

SALAD
- 6 cups baby kale, washed and dried

- 2 cups diced cooked chicken
- 2 celery ribs, diced
- ¾ cup thinly sliced red onion
- ½ cup walnuts, roughly chopped
- ½ cup dried cranberries
- ¼ cup crumbled feta cheese

1. *To make the dressing:* In a blender, add the white wine vinegar, lemon juice, Dijon mustard, honey, garlic, oregano, salt, and pepper. As it blends, pour in a steady stream of olive oil until the dressing comes together. Keep in the refrigerator until ready to use.

2. *To make the salad:* In a large bowl, lightly toss the kale, chicken, celery, red onion, walnuts, cranberries, and feta cheese. Toss with the dressing and serve.

MAN IN BLACK: But if there can be no arrangement, then
we are at an impasse.

VIZZINI: I'm afraid so—I can't compete with you physically.
And you're no match for my brains.

MAN IN BLACK: You're that smart?

VIZZINI: Let me put it this way: Have you ever heard
of Plato, Aristotle, Socrates?

MAN IN BLACK: Yes.

VIZZINI: Morons.

MAN IN BLACK: Really? In that case, I challenge you
to a battle of wits.

VIZZINI: For the Princess? To the death? I accept.

FEZZIK'S STRENGTH

Friends are like side dishes—it's nice to have a strong one by your side whose strengths are an asset to your dynamic. In the case of Fezzik, that can be taken both literally and figuratively. While he may be a formidable giant, his talent lies not only in his force but in his loyalty—a true stand-up guy whose mere presence brings the whole team together. These brussels sprouts are just like having Fezzik on your side—they're a perfect complement to a main dish, but they also make quite a statement all on their own.

MAKES 6 SERVINGS (GF, V+)

1½ pounds brussels
    sprouts, trimmed and
    halved
2 garlic cloves, minced
¼ cup olive oil

1½ tablespoons apple
    cider vinegar
1½ tablespoons packed
    light brown sugar
1 teaspoon kosher salt

½ teaspoon black pepper
3 tablespoons chopped
    pecans

1. Preheat the oven to 400°F. Prep a baking sheet with parchment paper.
2. In a large bowl, toss the brussels sprouts with the garlic, olive oil, apple cider vinegar, brown sugar, salt, and pepper. Spread out on the prepped baking sheet.
3. Bake for 40 minutes, until crisp.
4. Toss with the pecans and serve.

INIGO'S COURAGE

Inigo's bravery is unequaled. When it comes to working as a team, his fearlessness is emboldened by Westley's keen smarts and Fezzik's brawn. With everyone's strengths working together, there's no challenge they can't take on. Patatas bravas is a Spanish side dish that is perfectly fried, with just the right amount of added spice. These piquant potatoes are bold, dynamic, and the perfect accompaniment to bring out the best in your main dish. An ambrosial ode to Inigo's courageous spiritedness, its bold flavor will keep you coming back for more.

MAKES 4 SERVINGS (GF, V+)

SAUCE
1 tablespoon olive oil
1 small shallot, diced
2 garlic cloves, minced
1 tablespoon cornstarch

2 teaspoons sweet smoked paprika
1½ teaspoons hot smoked paprika
1 cup vegetable broth

POTATOES
1 pound russet potatoes
¼ cup vegetable oil
½ teaspoon salt
1 tablespoon minced fresh parsley

1. *To make the sauce:* In a small saucepan over medium heat, add the oil and cook the shallot and garlic for 2 to 3 minutes, until softened. Stir in the cornstarch and both paprikas.

2. Whisk in the vegetable broth and bring to a boil. Cook for 2 to 3 minutes, until thickened. Remove from the heat, and set aside.

3. *To prepare the potatoes:* Peel and cut the potatoes into 1-inch cubes. Place in a bowl of cold water for 20 minutes. Drain and pat completely dry.

4. In a large, deep skillet, heat the oil and add the potatoes. Cover and cook for 15 to 20 minutes, stirring every 5 minutes, until golden brown. Sprinkle with the salt.

5. Pour over the sauce, sprinkle with the parsley, and serve.

Queen of Slime

In Buttercup's dream, an ancient heckler throws insults at her faster than an R.O.U.S. running in a Fire Swamp. Being called the royal rubbish is a stinging barb, but being crowned the Queen of Slime wouldn't be all bad if you could spend your reign gobbling up this flavorful green dressing. Packed full of nutritious, virescent veg, this flavorful, creamy sauce works not only for salads but for gracefully dipping vegetables, quite the monarchal way of lunching. This delicious dip will turn your insulting nightmares into sweet dreams of being rescued.

MAKES 10 SERVINGS (GF, V)

1 cup fresh parsley
1 cup fresh spinach leaves
¼ cup minced fresh cilantro
1 garlic clove, peeled

2 tablespoons lemon juice
1 tablespoon white wine vinegar
½ cup vegetable oil

½ cup Greek yogurt
½ teaspoon kosher salt
¼ teaspoon black pepper
Sliced raw vegetables, for serving

In a blender, add the parsley, spinach, cilantro, garlic, lemon juice, vinegar, and oil. Blend until just combined. Add the Greek yogurt, salt, and pepper. Blend until smooth. Serve with the vegetables.

THE ANCIENT BOOER: Booo!

BUTTERCUP: Why do you do this?

THE ANCIENT BOOER: Because you had love in your hands, and you gave it up.

BUTTERCUP: But they would have killed Westley if I hadn't done it.

THE ANCIENT BOOER: Your true love lives and you marry another. True love saved her in the Fire Swamp, and she treated it like garbage. And that's what she is, the Queen of Refuse! So, bow down to her if you want. Bow to her. Bow to the Queen of Slime, the Queen of Filth, the Queen of Putrescence. Boo! Boo! Rubbish! Filth! Slime! Muck! Boo! Boo!

Anybody Want a Peanut?

Fezzik's rock-throwing skills are rivaled only by his ability to throw down rhymes. It's a skill that drives Vizzini crazy, but it's truly awe-inspiring. To chop up verses with poetic patterns is a true skill that not everyone has. You could say that it's his greatest strength next to his actual strength. Fezzik's ability to rhyme makes him endearing and trustworthy, the ideal comrade in arms. Like his rhapsodic verses, this recipe for peanut candy is quite dandy. They're simply sublime; try them anytime!

MAKES 4 SERVINGS (GF, V+)

2 cups roasted
   unsalted peanuts
1 cup granulated sugar

⅓ cup water
½ teaspoon vanilla extract

¼ teaspoon ground
   cinnamon
¼ teaspoon kosher salt

1. Prep a baking sheet with parchment.
2. In a large skillet, stir together the peanuts, sugar, and water. Turn the heat to medium and cook, stirring constantly, for 2 minutes, until the sugar begins to crystallize.
3. As the sugar begins to dry, lower the heat and continue to stir the peanuts into the syrup, until golden brown, about 25 minutes. Add the vanilla, cinnamon, and salt, stirring to coat.
4. Pour out onto the prepped baking sheet and let cool completely before serving.

INIGO: Fezzik, are there rocks ahead?

FEZZIK: If there are, we'll all be dead.

VIZZINI: No more rhymes now, I mean it.

FEZZIK: Anybody want a peanut?

Chapter Five

Valiant Desserts

There is nothing in the world quite as magical as dessert. It's something to look forward to at the end of a meal, and choosing which one will conclude a fabulous dinner can be just as important as the main dish itself. From cookies to cakes, pies to ice cream, the choices are endless. Like true love, the right dessert will seek you out, and when you know, you just know.

BUTTERCUP: I fear I'll never see you again.

WESTLEY: Of course you will.

BUTTERCUP: But what if something happens to you?

WESTLEY: Hear this now: I will come for you.

BUTTERCUP: But how can you be sure?

WESTLEY: This is true love. You think this happens every day?

Dessert recipes tend to be the ones that family members remember most. Many are handed down from generation to generation, each with their own special something that makes them memorable. Valerie knew the power of sweets by coating her Miracle Max pills in candy—it's the chocolate coating that makes it go down easier. If you've gotta go, death by chocolate isn't half bad.

Like a good story, some dessert recipe origins may be a bit muddled, but everyone remembers how they tasted. And not being able to replicate them exactly only makes them that much better—adding personal flair is what makes a generational dessert special.

These sweet endings are a treasure of memories, the flavors that take you back to your childhood, your first love, or your first adventure. Desserts feel like a cure-all, a fix for any situation that has us frightened, angry, weepy, or lovelorn. There's no better way to cope than with dessert; it's the perfect fairy-tale ending.

Farm Fresh Pie

Raised on a small farm in the country of Florin, Buttercup was surrounded by all the homestead essentials when it came to making farm-to-table meals. This custard pie uses the freshest eggs, milk, butter, and cream; it's a veritable dairy-filled heaven in pie form. A simple custard pie is like an unexpected relationship, when you out find the perfect thing was right in front of you the whole time. This delicious dessert is so easy to make, you won't even need a farm boy to help.

— MAKES 10 SERVINGS (V) —

CRUST
1½ cups all-purpose flour
¼ teaspoon ground cinnamon
¼ teaspoon kosher salt
4 tablespoons (½ stick) cold unsalted butter, cubed

¼ cup vegetable shortening
4 tablespoons ice water
1 large egg white, lightly beaten

CUSTARD
1½ cups whole milk

1 cup heavy cream
¼ teaspoon kosher salt
3 large eggs
¾ cup granulated sugar
1 tablespoon vanilla extract
¼ teaspoon ground nutmeg

1. *To make the crust:* In a large bowl, whisk together the flour, cinnamon, and salt. Add the butter and shortening, working them in together until crumbly. Sprinkle in the water, 1 tablespoon at a time, working it into the dough until just combined.

2. Wrap the dough in plastic wrap and chill in the refrigerator for 40 minutes.

3. Preheat the oven to 375°F. Grease a pie pan with nonstick spray.

4. Roll out the dough into a 13-inch circle and place in the prepped pie pan. Crimp the edges. Line the pie crust with parchment and fill with pie weights. Bake for 20 minutes. Remove the pie weights and discard the parchment. Brush with the egg white and bake for another 10 minutes, until golden brown. Let cool completely.

5. *To make the custard:* Turn the oven temperature down to 300°F.

6. In a large saucepan over medium heat, add the milk, heavy cream, and salt. When bubbles start to form around the edges, turn off the heat and set aside.

7. In a large bowl, whisk the eggs and sugar. Temper the mixture by adding ½ cup of the hot milk mixture to the eggs, whisking constantly. Pour the egg mixture into the hot milk, stirring constantly.

8. Pour the custard through a sieve, then stir in the vanilla.

9. Carefully pour the filling into the pie crust. Sprinkle with the nutmeg, then cover the edges of the pie with aluminum foil. Bake for 40 minutes, until the custard is just set.

10. Let the pie cool completely, then refrigerate until ready to serve.

Bread Pirate Roberts

There is no more feared looter on the seas than the Dread Pirate Roberts. While you may think naming a sugared, ambrosial, croissant and chocolate-filled sweet treat after such a loathsome monster is too placid, fear not! This dessert is as rich and captivating as its namesake. You see, this bread pudding is not delicate in the slightest. After all, once word leaks out that a pirate has gone soft, people begin to disobey you, and then it's nothing but work, work, work, all the time.

— MAKES 8 SERVINGS (V) —

6 butter croissants, cubed

2 tablespoons unsalted butter, melted

½ cup chocolate chips

4 large eggs, beaten

2 cups half-and-half

2 cups heavy cream

½ cup packed light brown sugar

1 teaspoon ground cinnamon

¼ teaspoon kosher salt

2 teaspoons vanilla extract

1. Preheat the oven to 350°F. Prep an 8–inch round baking dish with nonstick spray. Add the croissants and toss with the butter and chocolate chips.
2. In a large bowl, whisk the eggs, half-and-half, heavy cream, brown sugar, cinnamon, salt, and vanilla. Pour over the croissants.
3. Place the baking dish on a baking sheet and bake for 45 minutes, until golden brown. Serve.

INIGO: Who are you?!

MAN IN BLACK: No one of consequence.

INIGO: I must know.

MAN IN BLACK: Get used to disappointment.

INIGO: Okay.

PIT OF DESPAIR

The Pit of Despair is not a place you ever want to find yourself. Torture is obviously unpleasant, and who's got time for that? When it comes to agonizing pain, you should only have to deal with such anguish when choosing a dessert. This molten crème brûlée is anything but torture—in fact, you could say it's next-level nirvana. A thick chocolate cream encased in a magical shell of sweet caramelized sugar, just waiting to be cracked open. When it comes to torment, this a dessert worth dying for.

MAKES 6 SERVINGS (GF, V)

CUSTARD
2 cups half-and-half
1 cup heavy cream
1 teaspoon instant espresso powder
½ teaspoon vanilla extract

¼ teaspoon kosher salt
⅔ cup semi-sweet chocolate
4 large egg yolks
⅓ cup granulated sugar

TOPPING
6 teaspoons granulated sugar, divided
6 mint leaves
6 raspberries

1. *To make the custard:* Preheat the oven to 300°F.

2. In a large saucepan, add the half-and-half, heavy cream, instant espresso powder, vanilla, and salt. Bring to a boil. Remove from the heat and stir in the chocolate, until smooth.

3. In the bowl of an electric mixer, mix the egg yolks and sugar on low speed. Slowly mix in the chocolate mixture.

4. Sieve the custard into a separate bowl. Spoon into 6 individual ramekins.

5. Place the ramekins in a 13 x 9–inch baking dish. Fill the pan with hot water, about halfway up the ramekins. Carefully transfer to the oven and bake for 40 to 45 minutes, until just set and slightly jiggly.

6. Let cool to the touch, then remove the ramekins from the water bath and refrigerate for 3 hours. Cover with plastic wrap and continue to refrigerate overnight.

7. *To add the topping:* When ready to serve, sprinkle 1 teaspoon sugar over each custard. Use a kitchen torch to caramelize the sugar for a few seconds, until it turns a golden brown. Add a mint leaf and raspberry to each and serve.

WESTLEY: Where am I?

THE ALBINO: The Pit of Despair. Don't even think—don't even think about trying to escape. The chains are far too thick. And don't dream of being rescued either. The only way in is secret. And only the Prince, the Count, and I know how to get in and out.

WESTLEY: Then I'm here till I die?

THE ALBINO: Till they kill you. Yeah.

WESTLEY: Then why bother curing me?

THE ALBINO: The Prince and the Count always insist on everyone being healthy before they're broken.

WESTLEY: So it's to be torture.

LIGHTNING SAND PUDDING

The Fire Swamp certainly has its downsides, with Lightning Sand being pretty high on the list of dangers you'd want to avoid. It will trap you out of nowhere, unexpected, frightening, all-consuming—it's not something you can prepare for. While the real Lightning Sand is generally unpleasant, these little pudding cups are anything but. An ode to the swamp's nightmarish death trap, these are sweet puddings layered with a crumbly cookie topping that will capture your sweet tooth and never let go. They're downright delightful as far as hazards go.

MAKES 6 SERVINGS (V)

COOKIE LAYER
1 cup vanilla wafers
½ cup graham crackers

TAPIOCA PUDDING
2¾ cups whole milk
1 large egg

⅓ cup granulated sugar
3 tablespoons quick-cooking small pearl tapioca
1½ teaspoons vanilla extract
¼ teaspoon salt

VANILLA MOUSSE
1 box (3.4 ounces) vanilla pudding mix
1 cup whole milk
8 ounces frozen whipped topping, thawed

1. *To make the cookie layer:* In a food processor, grind the vanilla wafers and graham crackers into fine crumbs. Set aside.

2. *To make the tapioca pudding:* In a medium saucepan over medium heat, whisk the milk, egg, sugar, and tapioca. Bring to a boil. Remove from the heat and stir in the vanilla and salt.

3. Spoon the tapioca pudding into six parfait glasses, and refrigerate for 30 minutes.

4. *To make the vanilla mousse:* In a large bowl, whisk together the vanilla pudding mix and milk for 2 minutes, until thickened.

5. Fold in the thawed whipped topping. Spoon on top of the tapioca layer.

6. Refrigerate for 1 hour or until ready to serve.

7. Sprinkle with the crushed cookies and serve.

Twoo Wove's Kiss Cookies

It's easy to want to skip to the end when the clergyman goes on and on about wove, twoo wove, but like these cookies, it will fowwow you fowever. Since the invention of the kiss, there have been five kisses that were rated the most passionate, the most pure. And these cookies are right up there, maybe a close sixth in line. While the Grandson may have an aversion to kissing scenes, perhaps these confections will change his mind. Crumbly and sweet, filled with a sweet dollop of chocolate, these cookies will inspire you to tweasure your wove.

MAKES 30 COOKIES (V)

1 cup (2 sticks) unsalted
  butter, softened
½ cup granulated sugar
1 teaspoon vanilla extract

2 cups all-purpose flour
¼ teaspoon ground
  cinnamon
¼ teaspoon kosher salt

30 chocolate kiss candies
1½ cups confectioners'
  sugar, divided

1. In the bowl of an electric mixer, cream the butter, sugar, and vanilla for 5 minutes, until fluffy.
2. Stir in the flour, cinnamon, and salt until just combined. Refrigerate the dough for 1 hour.
3. Preheat the oven to 375°F. Shape the dough into 1-inch balls. Flatten and place a chocolate kiss in the center of each, then pinch up the dough to cover the kiss. Place 2 inches apart on two baking sheets.
4. Bake for 12 minutes. Let cool slightly on a wire rack for 5 minutes.
5. Roll the cookies in the confectioners' sugar. Let cool completely before serving.

Miracle Max's Miracle Pills

Humperdinck! Humperdinck! Humperdinck! When it comes to true love, Valerie will do all she can to coerce Max to help. His resistance is understandable. After all, bringing someone back who is mostly dead is no easy task—especially when your confidence is shattered. But if anyone can work together to make a reanimation pill, it's Max and Valerie. These pills won't bring you back from the half-dead, but they're sure to perk you up. The chocolate coating makes it go down easier but doesn't change the fact that the Prince is the King's stinking son.

—————— MAKES 15 SERVINGS (V) ——————

BROWNIES
¾ cup (1½ sticks) unsalted butter, melted
1 cup granulated sugar
½ cup packed light brown sugar
3 large eggs
1 tablespoon strong brewed coffee
1 teaspoon vanilla extract
1 cup all-purpose flour
¾ cup cocoa powder
½ teaspoon baking powder
¼ teaspoon salt

TRUFFLES
6 ounces mascarpone cream
1 pound dark chocolate, roughly chopped

1. *To make the brownies:* Preheat the oven to 350°F. Prep an 8 x 8-inch baking pan with nonstick spray.

2. In a large bowl, whisk the butter, granulated sugar, brown sugar, eggs, coffee, and vanilla.

3. Stir in the flour, cocoa powder, baking powder, and salt, until just combined.

4. Pour into the prepped baking pan and bake for 25 to 30 minutes, until just set. Let cool completely.

5. *To make the truffles:* Prep a baking sheet with parchment. In a large bowl, crumble the cooled brownies and fold in the mascarpone. Use a 2-inch scoop to create large balls and place on the prepped baking sheet. Freeze for 30 minutes to 1 hour.

6. In a double boiler, melt the dark chocolate. Dip the truffle balls into the melted chocolate, then place back on the parchment-lined baking sheet. Freeze until ready to serve.

INIGO: That's a miracle pill?

VALERIE: The chocolate coating makes it go down easier. But you have to wait fifteen minutes for full potency. And you shouldn't go swimming after, for at least, what?

MIRACLE MAX: An hour.

VALERIE: Yeah, an hour.

MIRACLE MAX: A good hour. Yeah.

FLORIN'S 500TH ANNIVERSARY CAKE

When you have a country to run and allegiances start to waver, there's no better way to get the citizens on your side than to throw an extravagant party. Commemorating the anniversary of your nepotistic, inherited commonwealth should be a blowout full of food, drink, and hopefully no murder. Whether it's a wedding or a party to celebrate the 500th anniversary of your country, a beautiful, custard cream-filled charlotte russe is the perfect dessert for every occasion. Except for an assassination attempt—there's no cake for that.

MAKES 12 SERVINGS (V)

1 pound mascarpone cheese
2 cups confectioners' sugar
2 teaspoons vanilla extract

3 cups heavy cream
20 (5-inch) ladyfinger cookies
2 cups blackberries

2 cups blueberries
2 cups raspberries
¼ cup dark chocolate shavings

1. In a large bowl, stir together the mascarpone, confectioners' sugar, and vanilla. Set aside.

2. In the bowl of an electric mixer fitted with the whisk attachment, whip the heavy cream until stiff peaks form. Stir in the mascarpone mixture, until just combined.

3. Scoop 1 cup of the cream mixture into a piping bag and pipe around the interior edge of a 9-inch springform pan. Using the mascarpone to hold them in place, place 16 ladyfingers around the interior edge, standing them upright, rounded-side up and sugared-side facing out. Line the bottom of the pan with the remaining ladyfingers, breaking them up to fill in the gaps.

4. Scoop one-third of the remaining cream mixture into the pan, spreading evenly. Top with one-third of the berries, and then half of the chocolate shavings.

5. Add a layer of ladyfingers. Top with another one-third of the cream, one-third of the berries, and the remaining chocolate shavings.

6. Add a final layer of ladyfingers, then top with the remaining cream. Use the remaining berries to decorate the top.

7. Cover with plastic wrap and refrigerate for 5 hours, until set.

8. Unmold from the springform and place on a serving plate. Tie a ribbon around the outside to hold everything in place.

RUGEN: Now, where is that secret knot? It's impossible to find. Are you coming down into the Pit? Westley's got his strength back. I am starting him on The Machine tonight.

HUMPERDINCK: Tyrone, you know how much I love watching you work. But I've got my country's 500th anniversary to plan, my wedding to arrange, my wife to murder, and Guilder to frame for it. I'm swamped.

RUGEN: Get some rest—if you haven't got your health, you haven't got anything.

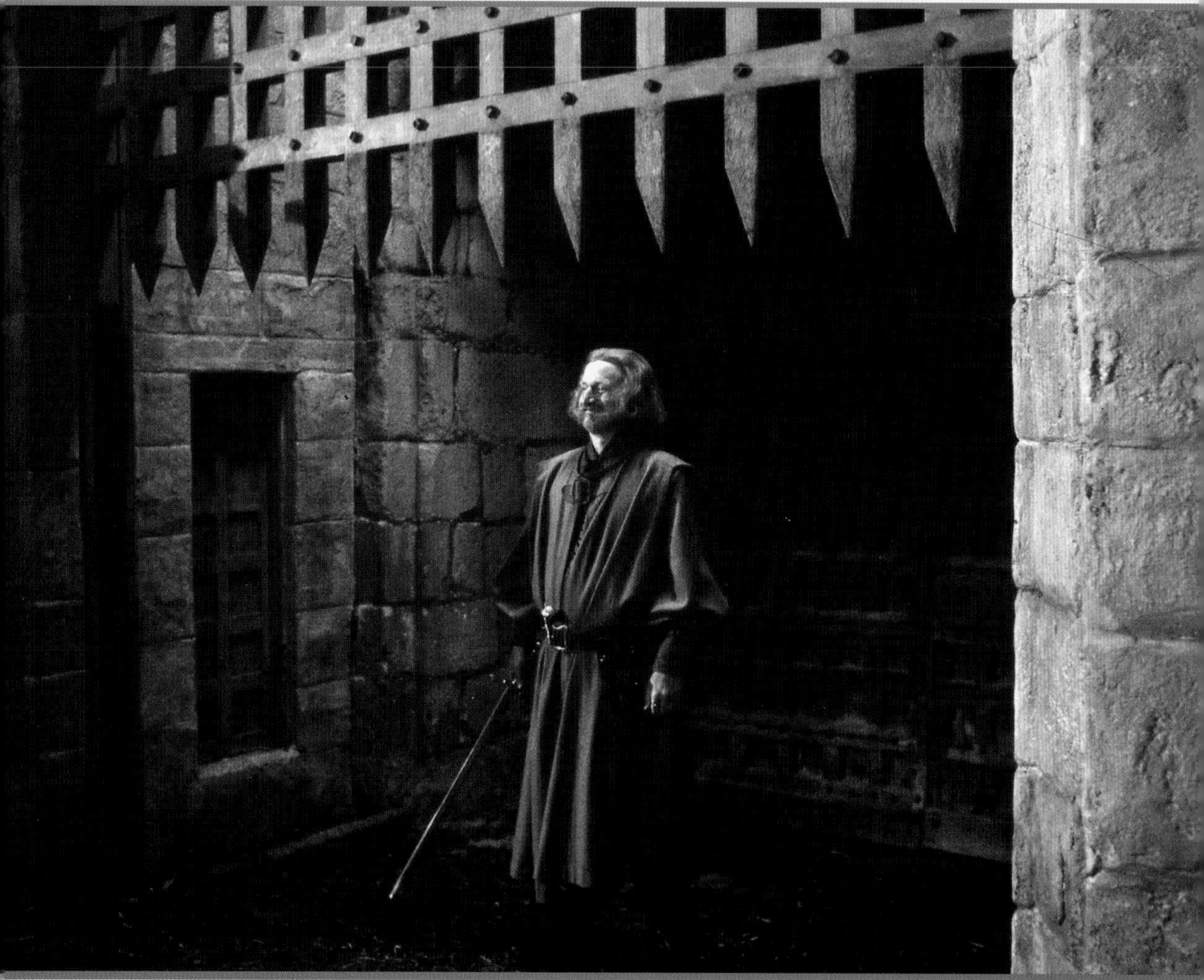

GATE KEY COOKIES

When you're on a mission and problems arise, you have to get inventive. It's a wonder what a wheelbarrow, holocaust cloak, and a little ingenuity can do. It can clear your path to your destination, I tell you what. And when you get there, the gate key is all you need to finish the job. These cookies are pressed shortbread, molded to look like the precious portcullis opener. However, these edible keys are much easier to acquire, and there are no hallucinatory scare tactics required.

WESTLEY: Give us the gate key.

YELLIN: I have no gate key.

INIGO: Fezzik, tear his arms off.

YELLIN: Oh, you mean this gate key.

———————— MAKES 24 COOKIES (V) ————————

1 cup (2 sticks) unsalted butter, softened
½ cup packed light brown sugar
1 tablespoon confectioners' sugar

¼ teaspoon ground cinnamon
¼ teaspoon ground nutmeg
¼ teaspoon kosher salt
1 large egg

2 teaspoons vanilla extract
3 cups all-purpose flour
Special equipment: food-grade silicone key-shaped mold

1. In the bowl of an electric mixer, cream the butter, brown sugar, and confectioners' sugar, until light and fluffy.
2. Stir in the cinnamon, nutmeg, salt, egg, and vanilla, until just combined. Add the flour ½ cup at a time, until fully incorporated.
3. Divide the dough into 2 halves, wrap in plastic wrap, and refrigerate for 45 minutes to 1 hour.
4. Preheat the oven to 400°F. Prep two baking sheets with parchment.
5. On a lightly floured surface, roll out the dough to ¼ inch thick. Dust the mold with flour, then press into the dough. Remove the dough from the mold and place on the prepped baking sheets.
6. Bake for 10 to 12 minutes until light golden brown. Let cool completely before serving.

VALERIE'S MAGICAL FLAN

Valerie is not a witch; she's Max's wife! Ever since Prince Humperdinck fired Max, his confidence is shattered, but with Valerie by his side, together they can work miracles. Like Valerie and Max, this confection consists of cake and flan working together to perform magic right before your eyes. The cake batter goes in first, followed by the flan mixture, but while it cooks, the layers will magically switch places and you'll end up with a flan-topped cake. The process is bewitching but the flavor is enchanting, a magical miracle dessert you won't soon forget.

— MAKES 16 SERVINGS (V) —

CAKE

¼ cup caramel sauce
1½ cups all-purpose flour
½ cup cocoa powder
1 teaspoon baking powder
½ teaspoon baking soda
¼ teaspoon kosher salt

¾ cup (1½ sticks) unsalted butter
½ cup packed light brown sugar
½ cup granulated sugar
1 large egg
1 cup whole milk
¼ cup cold brewed coffee

FLAN

1 can (12 ounces) evaporated milk
1 can (14 ounces) sweetened condensed milk
4 large eggs
1½ teaspoons vanilla extract

1. *To make the cake:* Preheat the oven to 350°F. Prep a large Bundt pan with nonstick spray. Evenly pour the caramel sauce into the prepped pan. Set aside.

2. In a large bowl, whisk the flour, cocoa powder, baking powder, baking soda, and salt. Set aside.

3. In the bowl of an electric mixer, cream the butter, brown sugar, and granulated sugar for 2 to 3 minutes, until fluffy. Stir in the egg until combined.

4. Alternate adding the dry ingredients and the milk and coffee to the batter, until just combined.

5. Evenly pour the batter into the Bundt pan, covering the caramel sauce. Set aside.

6. *To make the flan:* In a separate large bowl, use a hand mixer to stir together the evaporated milk, sweetened condensed milk, eggs, and vanilla, until smooth. Pour over the cake batter.

7. Place the Bundt pan in a shallow baking pan and place in the oven. Fill the baking pan with hot water to create a water bath.

8. Bake for 1 hour. Remove the Bundt pan from the baking pan and let cool for 1 hour, then refrigerate for 2 hours. Run a knife around the edges, place a serving plate on top, then turn over and invert the cake onto the plate. Slice and serve.

VALERIE: LIAR!

MIRACLE MAX: Get back, witch!

VALERIE: I'm not a witch, I'm your wife. But after what you just said, I'm not even sure I want to be that anymore.

MIRACLE MAX: You never had it so good.

INIGO'S BRANDY SNAPS

When Vizzini first happened upon Inigo, he was so inebriated that he couldn't even buy brandy. Having been on the hunt for his father's killer for twenty years, he was starting to lose confidence. Plus, there's not a lot of money in the revenge business. That being said, a good brandy snap is always there to calm your worries. And there's no need for drinkable brandy to drown your sorrows when these cookies are available. Lacy and crisp with a creamy filling, they almost taste better than revenge. Almost . . .

MAKES 20 SERVINGS (V)

COOKIES
½ cup (1 stick) unsalted butter
½ cup packed light brown sugar
½ cup molasses

1 cup all-purpose flour
¼ teaspoon ground cinnamon
¼ teaspoon ground ginger
⅛ teaspoon kosher salt
2 teaspoons brandy

WHIPPED CREAM
1 cup heavy cream
½ teaspoon vanilla extract

1. *To make the cookies:* Preheat the oven to 325°F. Prep two baking sheets with parchment.
2. In a medium saucepan over low heat, stir the butter, brown sugar, and molasses, until melted.
3. In a large bowl, whisk together the flour, cinnamon, ginger, and salt. Make a well in the center of the dry ingredients and pour in the butter mixture and brandy. Stir together until well combined.
4. Scoop the dough by the tablespoon onto the prepped baking sheets.
5. Bake for 8 to 10 minutes, until lightly golden. Let sit for 2 minutes, then oil the handle of a wooden spoon and wrap each brandy snap around it, overlapping the edges to close. Let cool on a wire rack.
6. *To make the whipped cream:* In a medium bowl with a hand mixer, whip the heavy cream and vanilla until stiff peaks are formed. Scoop the cream into a piping bag fitted with a star tip. Pipe the cream into the end of each brandy snap before serving.

Chapter Six

Triumphant Drinks

In any good story, we boo the villains and raise a glass to our heroes—even if we're not quite sure which glass we should be drinking out of. In life, sharing a drink with a loved one can signify so much more than just thirst; it's about camaraderie, rejoicing in simple pleasures, and the joys of friendship. To simply not celebrate life's little victories would be inconceivable!

MAN IN BLACK: All right: Where is the poison? The battle of wits has begun. It ends when you decide and we both drink, and find out who is right and who is dead.

A good beverage is a cause for celebration, whether those triumphs are big or small. Toasting to the new year can be as meaningful as raising a glass to the end of a completed project—both are big events, depending on your perspective. Sometimes it's the little things that make the biggest impact, and those are certainly worth memorializing with a liquid refreshment.

While you may not be clinking glasses to a young Spaniard dedicating his life to avenging his father's death, sipping a well-earned beverage at the end of a long workweek is just as special.

Drinks are a tribute to the journey, from the seas, to the Fire Swamp, to swordplay, near-death experiences, and true love. Here's to the future, and to a bright, well-deserved happily ever after.

INCONCEIVABLE

Inconceivable! Some things defy all odds, prompting this repetitive exclamation from Vizzini. The Man in Black climbing up the Cliffs of Insanity, beating his giant, and besting his Spaniard. While this overused expression gets straight to the point, in more ways than one it's completely valid. It's inconceivable that Westley has such incomparable skills. When it comes to beverages, this shocking phrase must also be uttered at this colorful drink that changes color right before your eyes, like magic. Inconceivable!

MAKES 1 SERVING (GF, V+)

¼ teaspoon butterfly pea
  flower powder

1½ cups lemon-lime soda
2 tablespoons lemon juice

1 mint leaf

1. In a tall glass, add the butterfly pea flower powder and lemon-lime soda, stirring until dissolved.
2. Fill a glass with ice, then pour in the butterfly pea mixture. Pour in the lemon juice to change the color. Garnish with the mint leaf. Serve.

VIZZINI: He didn't fall? Inconceivable!
INIGO: You keep using that word—I do not think it means what you think it means.

GOOD NIGHT, WESTLEY

Westley's will to live for Buttercup is what fueled him through the nights aboard the Dread Pirate Roberts's ship, the Revenge. *Not knowing whether or not you're going to wake up alive is quite a burden, so a nice bedtime beverage is a good way to calm your nerves. This spiced nightcap is a heavenly dream made with real chocolate and a pinch of cinnamon for good measure. It's a mug of welcoming warm comfort that will lull you to sleep while you dream of true love.*

MAKES 1 SERVING (GF, V)

1 tablespoon cocoa powder, plus more for serving

2 teaspoons granulated sugar

¼ teaspoon ground cinnamon

1 cup whole milk, divided

2 ounces dark chocolate, chopped

Whipped cream, for serving

Cinnamon stick, for serving

1. In a small bowl, whisk the cocoa powder, sugar, and cinnamon with ¼ cup of the milk, until smooth. Set aside.

2. In a small saucepan over medium-high heat, pour in the remaining ¾ cup milk, chocolate, and cocoa powder mixture. Simmer and stir for 5 minutes, until combined and the chocolate has melted.

3. Pour into a mug and top with whipped cream. Dust with cocoa powder, add a cinnamon stick, and serve.

WESTLEY: This will all soon be but a happy memory because Roberts's ship, *Revenge*, is anchored at the far end. And I, as you know, am Roberts.

BUTTERCUP: But how is that possible, since he's been marauding twenty years and you only left me five years ago?

WESTLEY: I myself am often surprised at life's little quirks . . . You see, what I told you before about saying "please" was true. It intrigued Roberts, as did my descriptions of your beauty . . . Finally, Roberts decided something. He said, "All right, Westley, I've never had a valet. You can try it for tonight. I'll most likely kill you in the morning." Three years he said that. "Good night, Westley. Good work. Sleep well. I'll most likely kill you in the morning." It was a fine time for me. I was learning to fence, to fight, anything anyone would teach me. And Roberts and I eventually became friends.

Iocane Powder Punch

Iocane powder may be one of the world's most lethal toxins, but not to worry—simply spend years building up an immunity to it and you should be just fine. This drink is quite a bit less potent, as in not at all dangerous, which is much preferred. Instead, this is a dark red punch served in glasses rimmed with popping candy, which makes it just as exciting to drink with a far less deadly, and far happier, outcome.

MAN IN BLACK: Inhale this, but do not touch.

VIZZINI: I smell nothing.

MAN IN BLACK: What you do not smell is called iocane powder. It is odorless, tasteless, dissolves instantly in liquid, and is among the more deadly poisons known to man.

VIZZINI: Hmm.

—— MAKES 2 SERVINGS (GF, V+) ——

GLASSES
1 lime wedge
2 packets (0.33 ounces each) popping candy

PUNCH
½ cup pineapple juice
½ cup cranberry juice
1 cup ginger ale

1. *To prepare the glasses:* Run the lime around the rim of two glasses. Shake the popping candy onto a flat dish and turn the glasses over, twisting the rims into the popping candy. Set aside.
2. *To make the punch:* In a medium pitcher, stir together the pineapple juice and cranberry juice. Slowly stir in the ginger ale, so it doesn't bubble up.
3. Turn the glasses back over, fill with ice, pour the punch over, and serve.

Paper Cut
with Lemon Juice

When Inigo and Fezzik arrive at Miracle Max's hovel with a mostly dead Westley in tow, the old healer is shook. His lack of confidence is understandable as he feels he was wronged by the King's stinking son. Who can blame him? But it is possible to make lemons out of lemonade, especially when you have the ability to make miracles. This combination of lemon and lime is refreshing, restorative, and just might make you change your mind when it comes to helping out the noble cause of true love.

—— MAKES 6 SERVINGS (GF, V+) ——

SIMPLE SYRUP
1 cup granulated sugar
1 cup water

LEMON-LIMEADE
2 cups lemon juice
1 cup lime juice

3 cups cold water

1. *To make the simple syrup:* In a medium saucepan, stir together the sugar and water. Bring to a boil, stirring until the sugar dissolves. Let cool.
2. *To make the lemon-limeade:* In a large pitcher, stir together the lemon juice, lime juice, and cold water. Pour in the cooled simple syrup, and stir well.
3. Refrigerate until ready to serve. Pour over ice and serve.

INIGO: Are you the Miracle Max who worked for the King all those years?
MIRACLE MAX: The King's stinking son fired me. And thank you so much for bringing up such a painful subject. While you're at it, why don't you give me a nice paper cut and pour lemon juice on it? We're closed!

STORMING THE CASTLE

Valerie and Max's rallying salutation, "Bye-bye, boys!" "Have fun storming the castle!" sending off the trio of Inigo, Fezzik, and Westley, is a cheery yet ominous farewell. After all, it would take a miracle for them to pull off their radical plan. But this skilled team is determined, and nothing can stop them. This dark rum and ginger beer concoction tastes like a journey on the high seas with a splash of revenge. It will keep you going even when the chips are down, the ideal liquid refreshment for a squad of friends out for retribution.

MAKES 1 SERVING (V+)

4 ounces cold ginger beer ½ ounce fresh lime juice
2 ounces dark rum 1 lime wedge

Fill a highball glass with ice. Pour in the ginger beer. Pour over the dark rum, then the lime juice. Stir, garnish with the lime wedge, and serve.

INIGO: Thank you for everything.

MIRACLE MAX: Okay.

VALERIE: Bye-bye, boys.

MIRACLE MAX: Have fun storming the castle.

VALERIE: Think it'll work?

MIRACLE MAX: It would take a miracle. Bye!

INIGO MONTOYA'S TASTE OF REVENGE

"Hello. My name is Inigo Montoya. You killed my father. Prepare to die." Having searched for his father's killer for twenty years, Inigo doesn't hesitate when he finally comes face-to-face with Count Rugen. Such a confrontation was a long time coming, and now that he's bested his sworn enemy, he can finally rest. What comes next? Perhaps sip a relaxing glass of fruity spiked punch. Having been in the revenge business for so long, what will Inigo do for the rest of his life? Perhaps piracy? But first, sangria.

MAKES 6 SERVINGS (GF, V+)

2 tablespoons granulated sugar
1 cup orange juice
¼ cup brandy
¼ cup lemon juice

1 medium orange, sliced
1 medium lemon, sliced
1 plum, pitted and cubed
¾ cup blackberries, divided

1 bottle (750ml) dry red wine
6 sprigs fresh rosemary

1. In a large pitcher, stir together the sugar, orange juice, brandy, and lemon juice until the sugar is dissolved. Add the orange slices, lemon slices, plum, and all but 6 of the blackberries.

2. Pour in the red wine and place in the refrigerator until ready to serve.

3. Fill six glasses with ice, then pour over the sangria. Garnish each glass with a rosemary sprig and a blackberry skewered with a toothpick, and serve.

INIGO: My name is Inigo Montoya.
You killed my father. Prepare to die.

SEA WATER

The sea is where Westley set sail to find his fortune. The sea is what divides Florin and Guilder. The sea is where the Dread Pirate Roberts reigns. It's a wild and reckless place, but its pull cannot be denied. Like a tall glass of this sweet and creamy combo, it's dangerously addictive in the best way. Sipping this sweet sea water will take you right back to being aboard a ship, bobbing among the waves. This beautifully blue beverage is an ode to the sweet siren call of the sea.

MAKES 1 SERVING (GF, V)

1 cup sparkling water

2 teaspoons blue curacao syrup

2 tablespoons sweetened condensed milk

Into a tall glass, pour the sparkling water. Stir in the blue curacao syrup. Add ice to fill. Top with the sweetened condensed milk and serve.

PIRATE'S PUNCH

WESTLEY: Well, Roberts had grown so rich, he wanted to retire. So he took me to his cabin and told me his secret. "I am not the Dread Pirate Roberts," he said. "My name is Ryan. I inherited this ship from the previous Dread Pirate Roberts, just as you will inherit it from me. The man I inherited it from was not the real Dread Pirate Roberts, either."

Learning the ways of a pirate's life is more than just singing sea shanties and drinking heaps of rum, although that's a big part of it. But assuming the duties and becoming the leader of a lawless pirate brigade is another. Westley took on the challenge with aplomb, knowing full well that the journey would eventually lead him back to Buttercup. One sip of this rum-spiked horchata and you, too, will be fit to take over the Dread Pirate Roberts's mantle in no time, if you dare . . .

MAKES 6 SERVINGS (GF, V)

5 cups water
1 cup uncooked long-grain white rice
4 cinnamon sticks, plus more for garnish

1 star anise, plus more for garnish
1 can (12 ounces) evaporated milk

⅔ cup sweetened condensed milk
¼ cup rum
1 teaspoon vanilla extract

1. In a blender, add the water and rice. Blend until the rice is finely ground, 2 to 3 minutes. Pour the mixture into a large bowl along with the cinnamon sticks and star anise. Soak overnight in the refrigerator.

2. Sieve the rice water into a serving pitcher, discarding the rice, cinnamon sticks, and star anise. Stir in the evaporated milk, sweetened condensed milk, rum, and vanilla until combined. Refrigerate until ready to serve.

3. Pour over ice, garnish each glass with a cinnamon stick and star anise, and serve.

VIZZINI: But it's so simple. All I have to do is divine from what I know of you. Are you the sort of man who would put the poison into his own goblet, or his enemy's? . . . Now, a clever man would put the poison into his own goblet, because he would know that only a great fool would reach for what he was given. I'm not a great fool, so I can clearly not choose the wine in front of you. But you must have known I was not a great fool; you would have counted on it, so I can clearly not choose the wine in front of me.

MAN IN BLACK: You've made your decision then?

VIZZINI: Not remotely. Because iocane comes from Australia, as everyone knows. And Australia is entirely peopled with criminals. And criminals are used to having people not trust them, as you are not trusted by me. So I can clearly not choose the wine in front of you.

MAN IN BLACK: Truly, you have a dizzying intellect.

VIZZINI: Wait till I get going! Where was I?

Dizzying Intellect

In the Battle of Wits, Vizzini becomes understandably flustered—after all, Westley is a master when it comes to intellectual challenges. While the Sicilian uses his best diversion tactics, Westley sees right through the ruse and knows he has the upper hand. The dizzying display of Vizzini's mental spiral is as bubbly and refreshing as an Aperol spritz. His tactical repartee and rapid wordplay are just a distraction. Like this sparkling orange aperitif, it will spin your head and tickle your senses; it's bewildering to watch but at the same time refreshingly satisfying.

MAKES 1 SERVING (GF, V+)

3 ounces dry prosecco
2 ounces Aperol

1 ounce sparkling water
1 orange slice

Add ice to a wineglass, pour in the prosecco, add the Aperol, and finish with the sparkling water. Stir. Garnish with the orange slice and serve.

THE ALBINO

In the Pit of Despair it's the Albino's job to nurse Westley back to health. Why? Because the Prince and the Count always insist on everyone being healthy before they're broken. True torture. If one's to be made comfortable before facing their fate, having a drink in hand will surely make all the difference. As pale as the Albino himself, this frosty blend of tantalizing coconut cream is what takes this margarita to the next level. A truly refreshing aperitif that will distract you from the torture that lies ahead.

—————————— MAKES 1 SERVING (GF, V+) ——————————

GLASSES
1 lime wedge
Kosher salt

MARGARITA
½ cup ice
1½ ounces coconut cream
1½ ounces fresh lime juice

1½ ounces tequila
¾ ounce agave
¾ ounce Cointreau

1. *To prepare the glasses:* Run the lime wedge around the rim of a glass. Dip the edge of the glass in kosher salt. Set aside.

2. *To make the margarita:* Fill the base of a shaker with the ice. Add the coconut cream, lime juice, tequila, agave, and Cointreau. Shake vigorously for 1 minute. Pour into the salt-rimmed glass and serve.

Chapter Seven

Momentous
Soirées

hen a story ends, you want to capture that feeling forever. The adventurous highs and lows, the sad moments and the happy, the frightening cliffhangers and the joyous endings. Keeping memories and sentiments alive is what parties are for. You can capture a moment in time and celebrate it forever.

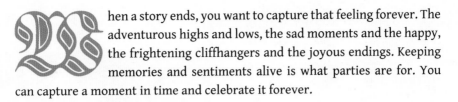

THE GRANDFATHER: Now I think you ought to go to sleep.

THE GRANDSON: Okay.

THE GRANDFATHER: Okay. All right. So long.

THE GRANDSON: Grandpa? Maybe you could come over and read it again to me tomorrow.

THE GRANDFATHER: As you wish.

Whether you're creating a large gathering or an intimate moment for two, putting together a festive affair can evoke the emotions of what you're celebrating and create new ones. It's these times in our lives that we celebrate that make life exciting. From the decor to playing a certain song, the mood is set by the choices you make. Picking out what to serve is just as important. Do you want your guests to mingle or to be focused? Should they be sitting with a bowl in hand or walking around with finger food talking to others? All of these factors are important when setting the stage for your social function.

Like the Grandfather recounting the story that's been told in the family for generations, the most important thing about the event you throw is the memories. You want your guests to relive the conversations and spirit of the moment, so that it will be a fond memory they'll want to experience over and over again.

Princess Bride Picnic

To create the perfect picnic on the grassy highlands of Florin, you'll want to gather the necessities for a lovely outdoor meal with a seaside view. All of these delicious treats are easily made in advance of your day out and are effortlessly portable for strolling along the rolling hills. Just be careful you don't accidentally take a tumble. In a large picnic basket, preferably one big enough for a giant to carry on his back, pack some alfresco essentials, including a beautiful tablecloth, preferably not in the colors of Guilder, and two goblets, just in case a battle of wits ensues.

◈ Start off your peaceful picnic with Buttercup Buttermilk Scones (page 9), a reminder of the farm and where it all began.

◈ Follow with Six-Fingered Sandwiches (page 37), since revenge is a dish best served cold and in the form of cucumbers and dill.

◈ Valerie's Portable Pocket Pies (page 88) are filled with savory meat and vegetables, and are ideal for toting along the shore on a swashbuckling adventure.

◈ Queen of Slime (page 100) dip and veggies provide the perfect side when you're worried about your future.

◈ Twoo Wove's Kiss Cookies (page 117) represent the dessert ending you've been waiting for all your life.

◈ It may seem unimaginable but a glass of Inconceivable (page 135) is the way to toast to surviving the most unlikely of trials and tribulations.

FLORIN'S ANNIVERSARY PARTY BUFFET

Planning the 500th anniversary party for the country of Florin could be a massive undertaking, but it doesn't have to be. Simply gather a few not-at-all suspicious hired hands to help carry out the event of the year. Add a few bite-sized appetizers and a strong celebratory swill and you've got yourself a quincentenary fête to remember! Hang a map of Florin and the royal coat of arms, in honor of the Prince and newly crowned Princess, above a long table, upon which place:

◈ A mountainous platter of The Giant's Boulders (page 47), because guests are easy to please when it comes to cheese. This rhyming . . . it comes with ease.

◈ Appetizer-sized skewers of Bonetti's Defense (page 64) also come in handy in case of a possible coup during the party.

◈ A stunningly large dish of the Spaniard's Paella (page 70) makes for a glorious seafood centerpiece.

◈ Pass around bubbly glasses of Dizzying Intellect (page 153) for toasting and drinking to another five hundred years of excellence.

◈ Finally, the pièce de résistance, Florin's 500th Anniversary Cake (page 121) is a glorious gâteau encased in regal ladyfingers, filled with velvety cream, and crowned with fresh berries, fit for the most regal of royal celebrations.

Thieves' Forest Happy Hour

After a long day of clearing out all the inhabitants of the forest, the Brute Squad needs to take a break, reassess, and wind down with a good drink and some apps. A Thieves' Forest happy hour is the perfect way to decompress and not have to worry about carrying out any more of Humperdinck's orders. You may need a wheelbarrow to safely transport all of these noshes and nibbles into a nice hovel, but as long as your torches are lit, you should be able to find your way.

❖ Every good drink requires a tasty bar snack, and Anybody Want a Peanut? (page 103) is the ideal crunchy accompaniment.

❖ Grab a slice of Thieves' Forest Flatbread (page 76) after you take one last sweep of undesirables.

❖ It's always good to have a wingman during a raid—not just a person who has your back, but someone who arrives with a plate piled high of Have You the Wing (page 87) succulent chicken wings.

❖ When raising a glass to a job well done, sipping spiked horchata Pirate's Punch (page 150) hits the spot after a hard day.

❖ Gathering the Brute Squad for a round of The Albino (page 154) coconut margaritas makes the job of chasing down malcontents even better.

 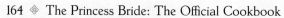

MARRIED COUPLE'S STAY-AT-HOME DATE NIGHT

Being married and working together can take a toll on a relationship, even one that's built on magic. After years of marriage, you can still find romance in a simple meal at home. Even the tiniest of dwellings can become a comfy, cozy setting for a delightful night in. Start by setting the mood with a flickering fire that can double as energy to boil up some magic potions (if necessary).

⟡ When it's just the two of you, a dark and stormy Storming the Castle (page 142) makes for a good starting aperitif.

⟡ Sharing simmering bowls of Fezzik's Stew (page 75) can help turn a cool evening into a warm and cuddly fireside meal.

⟡ Inigo's Courage (page 99), a bowl of tangy patatas bravas, is a tasty way to spice up a night at home.

⟡ If you slip up and call your wife a witch, a Good Night, Westley nightcap (page 136) of warm cinnamon hot chocolate will get you out of trouble.

⟡ Finishing a romantic dinner with a bite of chocolate makes a meal that much more magical. Miracle Max's Miracle Pills (page 118) are a magically sweet way to end the night.

⟡ It's always a good idea to have a pair of bellows at your side just in case an unexpected mostly dead person arrives on your doorstep to ruin your date night.

HEROES AND VILLAINS MOVIE NIGHT

A DIY dinner and a movie night can be a rollicking good time, especially when your guests get in on the action. Choose a fun flick that everyone will enjoy, then lean into it! Dress up, recite lines, and to truly ensure that a good time will be had by all, create a smorgasbord of easy-to-grab eats that will make couch dining and cleanup a dream. Before you pop the popcorn, remember that costumes aren't just for Halloween, so dress up as your favorite rhyming giant, an evil Prince, or go all out in robes befitting an Impressive Clergyman!

❖ A substantial sandwich will assist in getting you through the first act. An MLT (page 42) is a great starter as you're just settling in for the show.

❖ For guests who are so into the movie they don't even want to bother grabbing a plate, Valerie's Portable Pocket Pies (page 88) are easy to munch on as you choose the ideal seat for optimal viewing.

❖ If you need a quick bite of something sweet to eat without missing any of the action, Gate Key Cookies (page 125) are excellent for unlocking your cravings.

❖ Cheer the heroes! Boo the villains! Then toast to the climactic ending with a glass of Inigo Montoya's Taste of Revenge (page 145). Fruity sangria has an intoxicating way of bringing everyone together for a good time.

Index

Page numbers in italics refer to menus.

Acknowledgments

This book is for my mom, Alice Kawakami, who always instructs my kids to have fun storming the castle whenever they leave her house. To Kyle, Tyler, and Mason Fujikawa, who taught me that twoo wove does exist. To my brother Mark, who can rhyme even better than Fezzik, it must be . . . genetic. To my family who all believe that R.O.U.S.es exist, Chia-Ling Kawakami, Lori Okada and Pi Sao, Chad Okada and Shirley Jou, Becky and Joel Okada, Daniel and Alma Fujikawa, Tracey Fujikawa, Aidan, Gwen, Penelope, Hannah, and Kolten.

To Mel Caylo, Chrissy Dinh, and Sarah Kuhn, who I know would avenge me with as much voracity as Inigo Montoya, should the occasion arise. To the most supportive magic makers, who are always ready to bring me back to life with chocolate-coated Miracle Pills, Troy Benjamin, Cheryl deCarvalho, Chrys Hasegawa, Liza Palmer, and Mary Yogi. To Robb Pearlman—I will always say "As you wish" to any project we get to do together—thank you for having years of faith in me.

Lastly, to my kids: Bye-bye, boys. Have fun storming the castle.

About the Author

Photo by Shannon Cotrell

Jenn Fujikawa is a lifestyle and pop culture author, content creator, and host. Jenn is the author of multiple fandom-based books: *Parks and Recreation: The Official Cookbook*; *Star Wars: The Life Day Cookbook: Official Holiday Recipes From a Galaxy Far, Far Away*; *Gudetama: The Official Cookbook: Recipes for Living a Lazy Life*; *The I Love Lucy Cookbook: Classic Recipes Inspired by the Iconic TV Show*; and *The Goldbergs Cookbook*. She has created content for Disney, Ghostbusters, Lucasfilm, Marvel, and more. Unique family dinners and geeky baking are a staple of her website: justjennrecipes.com.